R.A.T. Fight:

Rapid Assault Tactics Used by Elite Forces to Survive Real-World Violence

PUBLISHED BY Arcana Horizons Editions

Arcana Horizons Editions – T. Dvorský

© **Copyright 2025 - All rights reserved.**

All introductions, analyses, and commentaries contained within this book may not be reproduced, duplicated, or transmitted without direct written permission from the author or the publisher. Under no circumstances will any blame or legal responsibility be held against the publisher or author for any damages, reparation, or monetary loss due to the information contained within this book, either directly or indirectly.

Legal Notice:

This book is only for personal use. You cannot amend, distribute, sell, use, quote, or paraphrase any part of the introductions, analyses, or commentaries within this book, without the consent of the author or publisher.

Disclaimer Notice:

Please note the information contained within this document is for educational and entertainment purposes only. All efforts have been executed to present accurate, up-to-date, reliable, complete information. No warranties of any kind are declared or implied. Readers acknowledge that the author is not engaged in the rendering of legal, financial, medical, or professional advice. The content within this book has been derived from various sources. Please consult a licensed professional before attempting any techniques outlined in this book.

By reading this document, the reader agrees that under no circumstances is the author responsible for any losses, direct or indirect, that are incurred as a result of the use of the information contained within this document, including, but not limited to, errors, omissions, or inaccuracies.

R.A.T. Fight

Table of contents

Introduction 4

Chapter 1: The Predator's Advantage 10

Chapter 2: The Warrior's Mindset 23

Chapter 3: Biomechanics of Destruction 34

Chapter 4: Close Quarters Combat Systems 45

Chapter 5: Tactical Use of Force Continuum 56

Chapter 6: Weapons of Opportunity 66

Chapter 7: Team Tactics and Group Dynamics 78

Chapter 8: Escape and Evasion 89

Chapter 9: Legal and Ethical Considerations 100

Chapter 10: Training and Skill Development 111

Conclusion: The Path Forward 121

Arcana Horizons Editions – T. Dvorský

Introduction

There is a truth that most civilized people, consciously or unconsciously, choose to ignore: the world remains a hunting ground. While we build cities, attend meetings, and sip our coffee in the illusion of safety, there are those who operate outside the moral code—predators who do not hesitate, who do not flinch, and who view your hesitation as an opportunity. In this battlefield of instinct and awareness, victory doesn't belong to the strongest or even the smartest—it belongs to the most prepared.

R.A.T. Fight: Rapid Assault Tactics was born not out of a fascination with violence, but out of necessity. In a world where confrontation can arrive without warning—in parking garages, ATMs, subway stations, or even your front porch—what separates the survivor from the victim is not always strength or size. It is awareness. It is mindset. It is preparation.

To understand violence is not to invite it. It is to stop pretending that good intentions offer protection. They don't. In nature, it is not the creature with the best moral compass that survives. It is the one that recognizes danger early, moves decisively, and finishes quickly.

This book does not glorify violence. It exposes it. It studies it. It prepares you for it. Because in the moment when your heart races, your breath shortens, and your vision narrows—when you're not sure whether you're about to be mugged, assaulted, or killed—you won't have time to philosophize. You will either act, or you will freeze. You will either prevail, or you will suffer.

The phrase *"The Predator's Advantage"* is not just a concept—it's an unfortunate reality. In every violent encounter, the attacker already has several layers of advantage: surprise, intent, and often, physical readiness. They've chosen the time. The place.

R.A.T. Fight

The target. You. Their plan is already unfolding by the time you even register something's wrong. Your only hope in that moment is to break their script—interrupt their plan—by being the one person who doesn't play the expected role of the compliant victim.

This book begins with a deep dive into how predators think, how they choose their targets, and how you—through body language, movement, and demeanor—are constantly broadcasting signals that either attract or deter violence. Whether you like it or not, every room you enter becomes a silent negotiation of power, intent, and perception. And whether you survive that negotiation depends less on luck and more on how well you've trained your instincts.

Criminals are not monsters with superpowers. But they are students of human behavior. They are hunters who have learned, through trial and error, which gazes to avoid and which shoulders to tap. They're experts at identifying vulnerability: the distracted shopper, the intoxicated pedestrian, the one staring at a phone, the one walking too close to a wall with no exit on the other side.

This is not paranoia—it is pattern recognition. And the sooner you learn the patterns, the sooner you stop being prey.

You might believe that you'll simply "know" when danger is near. That your gut will alert you. That your intuition will scream. Sometimes it does. But more often, those warnings are subtle—buried beneath social conditioning that tells us not to make a scene, not to assume the worst, not to "be rude." The attacker counts on that conditioning. It gives him time. Time to close distance. Time to test boundaries. Time to strike.

This is where the first major concept of *The Predator's Advantage* takes root: **The Interview Process**. Criminals often "interview" potential victims through subtle behavioral probes. A question about the time. A request for directions. An unnecessary compliment. These interactions are not innocent—they are data collection. The attacker is assessing your confidence, your reaction time, your awareness. Do you step back? Do you make eye contact? Do you look around? Do you hesitate? Every micro-behavior gives him information. And every piece of information either confirms his target—or convinces him to move on.

Most people fail these interviews because they don't know they're being tested. By the time they realize the encounter has gone sideways, it's too late. They're on the ground. They're bleeding. They're trapped. That is why *awareness*—not aggression—is your first weapon.

But awareness alone is not enough.

This book does not merely tell you to "be more aware." It teaches you **how**. From the Cooper Color Code to modern threat scanning protocols used by elite protection teams, you'll learn to categorize environments, people, and movements—creating real-time mental maps of normal behavior, so that anything abnormal becomes instantly obvious.

Why do some people seem to "sense" a fight before it begins? Why do some operators spot a tail on the street in five seconds while civilians don't notice it in five hours? It's not magic. It's baseline training. It's the ability to identify the rhythm of a place—whether it's a coffee shop or a parking lot—and detect the beat that doesn't belong.

Think of it like walking into your house and smelling gas. Even if you can't see the leak, you know something's wrong. That sense of wrongness is what this training gives you. And once you have it, you'll never walk into a room the same way again.

From there, we go deeper: into how to think and act under pressure. This is where the **OODA Loop**—Observe, Orient, Decide, Act—becomes your second lifeline. Originally developed by military strategist John Boyd, the OODA Loop is a mental framework for making decisions faster than your opponent can react. It has saved lives in combat zones, and it can save yours in a dark alley.

But here's the key: You can't learn the OODA Loop *during* an attack. You must train it beforehand. You must practice it so often that it becomes second nature—because in real violence, there is no time to analyze. There is only time to execute.

And execution is the ultimate goal of *Rapid Assault Tactics*.

What sets this book apart from generic self-defense manuals is its commitment to **realism**. This is not about flashy techniques or martial arts that crumble under adrenaline. This is not about memorizing hundreds of moves. This is about wiring your nervous system to respond with speed, aggression, and decisiveness when your life is on the line.

You'll learn how to recognize the *escalation triggers*—the precise moment when words are no longer just words. You'll discover the micro-expressions that precede violence: clenched jaws, dilating pupils, subtle shifts in posture that signal the storm about to hit. These are the cues that police officers and special forces operators study relentlessly—because missing them can be fatal.

And yet, this knowledge does not belong only to professionals. It belongs to you. To every man and woman who refuses to be helpless. To every parent, partner, and protector who understands that real safety comes not from hope, but from *readiness*.

You will not be trained to go looking for trouble. You will be trained to see it coming. To move before it hits. To *act* while others freeze.

This book is the result of years of study, cross-disciplinary research, and combatives distilled from military, law enforcement, and criminal psychology. Every concept has been vetted through the lens of reality: What works under stress? What breaks down? What can you count on when you're outnumbered, ambushed, or already wounded?

The coming chapters will walk you through:

- **How attackers profile their victims** and how you can shift your profile instantly;
- **How to read a room** like a protection agent scanning for threats;
- **How to move in confined spaces** while always knowing where your exits are;
- **How to integrate the OODA loop** into your decision-making so fluidly that you move before your attacker finishes his thought.

You won't just learn what to do. You'll learn *how to think*, *how to plan*, and *how to train* your body and mind to function as one unit. Violence is chaotic, but your response doesn't have to be.

This is where *The Predator's Advantage* ends—and your advantage begins.

The goal is not to become a predator yourself. It is to understand how predators operate so you can dismantle their game before it starts. It is to harden your mind, your body, and your presence to the point where the attacker sees you—and chooses someone else.

R.A.T. Fight

You will not win every fight. No one does. But after reading this book, you will never again be *unprepared*.

And that alone shifts the odds.
Now, let's begin.

Chapter 1: The Predator's Advantage

"The enemy gets a vote in every plan."
— General James Mattis

1.1 Understanding Criminal Psychology and Attack Patterns

There is no such thing as a random attack.

Though victims often describe acts of violence as sudden or unprovoked, the truth is that most predatory assaults are preceded by a process—a sequence of decisions and behaviors on the attacker's part that culminate in action. That process is often invisible to the untrained eye, but it leaves a trail. If you know what to look for, you can spot that trail early, long before the point of no return.

This chapter is about learning to think like the adversary. Not to emulate their malice, but to decode the strategies they use—because in the realm of personal defense, knowledge of the predator's playbook is your first real weapon.

Predatory Behavior Analysis

Predators, whether animal or human, follow patterns. They don't attack at random. They search for *opportunity*. They observe. They wait. They test.

In every environment, there are indicators that scream vulnerability. These cues can be visual, behavioral, or contextual.

To the trained eye, they're like neon signs pointing toward an easy win.

So, how does an attacker choose a victim?

First, body language.

The average criminal may not have a degree in psychology, but they are deeply attuned to human behavior—often because their livelihood or survival depends on it. They learn quickly, often through violent trial and error, what kind of body language signals strength… and what signals weakness.

Someone walking with their head down, shoulders slouched, eyes fixed on a phone—they're projecting disengagement. Someone walking with hesitant steps, avoiding eye contact, reacting nervously to proximity—these are red flags. They suggest a lack of confidence, a lack of awareness, and most importantly, *an unlikely threat*.

Predators subconsciously (or consciously) calculate risk vs. reward. They don't want a fair fight. They want the kind of target who will freeze, hesitate, or comply. An ideal victim isn't just physically smaller or weaker—they are mentally and emotionally unprepared.

Consider this: studies of violent offenders, including interviews with incarcerated criminals, have shown that many attackers can assess a potential victim's vulnerability within seconds—just by watching them walk. Stride length, gait rhythm, head movement, shoulder alignment—all of it contributes to the impression of someone who is either "in control" or "in trouble."

But beyond body language, environmental positioning also plays a key role.

The context in which someone is moving can amplify their vulnerability. A person walking alone at night, in poorly lit areas with few exits, is inherently more exposed than someone in a crowd. A person sitting with their back to the door in a public place—lost in headphones or conversation—may seem like a softer target than someone scanning the room periodically and keeping a clear view of exits.

Environmental vulnerability indicators are often invisible to the average person but crystal clear to those seeking advantage. They look for choke points, blind corners, obstructed sightlines. A predator's mind constantly scans for terrain advantages—places where they can corner, ambush, or flee with minimal resistance.

To combat this, you must learn to reverse the lens.

You must become the watcher of watchers.

When you enter a room or walk a street, ask yourself: If I were hunting someone, who would I pick? Why? What body language would catch my eye? What escape routes would I consider? Where are the blind spots? Then ask the hard question—do I fit the profile I just imagined?

By consciously examining how predators think, you begin to deconstruct your own habits, mannerisms, and patterns. You stop broadcasting weakness. You become a harder target before a confrontation even begins.

The Interview Process

Predators don't always strike without warning. In fact, many of them conduct an unspoken "interview" beforehand. This pre-attack ritual is used to test boundaries, gauge reactions, and assess resistance.

The interview can be subtle or overt. It might involve a stranger approaching with a question—"Do you have the time?" or "Can you help me find this address?" It might be a compliment that feels slightly off, or a joke made too early in an encounter. On the surface, these may seem like ordinary social interactions. But to a trained eye, they are probes.

The purpose of this probing is not conversation. It's evaluation.

The predator is watching how you respond. Do you look them in the eyes? Do you step back or hold your ground? Do you respond with clarity or with uncertainty? Do you glance around the environment, checking for others or for exits?

Each answer gives them more data.

Some interviews escalate in stages. If the first probe succeeds, the predator might push further—standing closer, asking a more invasive question, or using touch as a test. They are looking for one thing above all: *permission*. Not in the legal or ethical sense, but in the psychological one. They want to see whether you'll allow their escalation to continue unchecked.

In this sense, a confrontation doesn't begin with the first punch or the first shout—it begins the moment the boundary is crossed and not pushed back.

This is why many seasoned professionals train to respond to these interviews with calm but clear resistance. The response doesn't have to be aggressive. In fact, in many cases, aggression only escalates things unnecessarily. But it must be *firm*. An assertive "No, I'm good," delivered with eye contact and steady posture, is a far stronger deterrent than a fearful compliance.

The danger of the interview is that most people don't recognize it for what it is. Social conditioning teaches us to be polite, even when we feel uncomfortable. We're taught not to make assumptions, not to offend, not to judge. Predators exploit that hesitation. They use your decency as a shield.

Breaking that pattern starts with awareness. Once you learn to identify pre-assault interviews, you'll never experience them the same way again. You'll feel the difference between a genuine question and a manipulative probe. And more importantly, you'll respond from a place of control, not confusion.

Escalation Triggers and Micro-Expressions

Not all violent encounters begin with surprise. Some begin with words—arguments that shift suddenly, dramatically into assault.

Understanding the *escalation triggers* that turn verbal conflict into physical confrontation is essential for navigating those situations safely. There is a threshold in every heated interaction—a moment where posturing becomes action, where control is lost, and where danger becomes imminent.

But that threshold doesn't always shout. Often, it whispers.

The signs of an impending attack are subtle but predictable. They live in the body. In the breath. In the eyes.

A person about to launch an assault will often display involuntary micro-expressions—tiny, rapid muscle movements that escape conscious control. These might include:

- **Jaw clenching**: a rapid tightening of the facial muscles, often in preparation for aggression.

- **Lip compression**: lips pressed together hard and flat—often a sign of internal restraint or pending release.
- **Shoulder drop or weight shift**: unconscious adjustment of stance to prepare for movement.
- **Fist clenching or hand wringing**: signs of nervous energy channeling into potential action.
- **Eye aversion or stare-down**: depending on the person, either avoiding eye contact or maintaining it with unnatural intensity.

Then there are behavioral markers. The person might begin *blading* their body—turning slightly sideways to minimize their profile and prepare to strike. They might begin pacing, using motion to burn off adrenaline or to position themselves advantageously. Their voice may drop or rise suddenly. They might begin repeating themselves, losing rational coherence.

All of these are signs that the situation is escalating past words.

You must train yourself to detect these signs early—before the swing, before the grab, before the lunge. Because once the first blow lands, your ability to control the outcome is already compromised.

But perhaps most crucially, you must learn to identify *your own* escalation triggers. You must know what frustrates you, what frightens you, what causes you to freeze or lash out. The predator may not have your training—but they may know how to *press your buttons*. Your defense is only as strong as your ability to stay calm under pressure.

The predator thrives in environments where people are unaware, unprepared, and untrained. Their success depends not on brute force but on your predictability. Every signal you send—how you walk, how you stand, how you speak—tells them whether to move on or move in.

Understanding criminal psychology and attack patterns allows you to invert the dynamic. You cease to be a passive participant in your own safety. You become an active force—hard to read, harder to reach, and almost impossible to exploit.

Violence begins long before the first strike. But so does defense.

The coming sections will train you to assess environments like a professional, to construct mental maps that reveal danger before it strikes, and to orient yourself within the chaos of conflict using frameworks that have been battle-tested on every continent.

Because once you understand the predator, you stop being the prey.

1.2 Environmental Threat Assessment and Situational Awareness

Survival in violent encounters often hinges on what you do *before* the first move is made. It is not about reacting faster than your opponent—it is about *acting* before they realize you've seen them. This is the core of situational awareness: an evolving discipline that combines psychology, behavioral science, and tactical assessment to perceive threats in real-time while the rest of the world is still asleep at the wheel.

To begin, we must look at the foundational framework that underpins modern awareness training: the Cooper Color Code. Devised by Colonel Jeff Cooper, this system outlines four states of awareness—white, yellow, orange, and red. While most civilian self-defense courses stop here, in reality, elite security professionals operate with far greater nuance. Understanding the theory is one thing; applying it dynamically in fluid environments is quite another.

R.A.T. Fight

In condition white, a person is completely unaware, often lost in thought or distracted by a phone or internal monologue. Unfortunately, this is where most people spend their time—particularly in public settings. It is the most dangerous state to be in, because it invites ambush. In condition yellow, the practitioner is relaxed but alert. They are scanning their surroundings periodically, making mental notes without appearing paranoid. There is no identified threat, but awareness is active. This is the state we aim to live in—every day, in every environment.

Condition orange occurs when something changes. Perhaps a person's movement breaks the rhythm of the environment. Perhaps a car is parked where it shouldn't be, or someone enters a room and immediately scans it rather than walking directly to a seat. In orange, your mind identifies a potential threat and begins calculating responses. Not action yet—but preparation. And finally, condition red is execution. The threat is real. The decision to act has been made.

What separates professionals from the average citizen is the depth of their scanning process in conditions yellow and orange. Executive protection teams, for instance, develop mental scripts when entering new spaces. They examine entry points, surveillance blind spots, choke zones, and escape routes. They not only observe the people in the room but their relationships to the environment. Who is loitering without a purpose? Who keeps adjusting their jacket or bag? Who is walking too close? They are watching for breaks in pattern—and they are building baselines.

Baseline establishment is critical. In every setting—be it a café, airport, or parking lot—there exists a pattern of normalcy. The pace at which people walk, the volume of conversation, the typical flow of foot traffic. Once you understand what "normal" looks like in a particular space, it becomes much easier to spot "abnormal." A person standing still in a fast-moving crowd.

Someone walking against the grain in a way that doesn't align with their surroundings. An argument brewing in a location where people are usually quiet. These are data points that signal a potential breach of safety.

Establishing a baseline isn't about being hyper-vigilant; it's about being *tuned in*. Think of it like music. Once you know the melody, a wrong note stands out immediately. This principle is the same. By training your senses to register pattern, you give yourself a tactical edge that most people will never cultivate. You don't need to know what's wrong right away. You just need to know that *something* is wrong. And that recognition, even just two seconds ahead of everyone else, can be the difference between survival and catastrophe.

But awareness must be paired with movement. No matter how perceptive you are, if you don't have an escape plan, you're stuck. One of the greatest errors civilians make in dangerous situations is not identifying their exits—either because they assume they won't need them, or because they panic when threat arises. The difference in how military and protection personnel approach confined environments is stark: they *never* enter without calculating at least three exit options. These exits aren't always doors. They could be windows, stairwells, alleyways, service corridors. The key is pre-identification.

Maintaining 360-degree awareness means never fixating too long on one area. It means periodically checking your six, keeping mirrors and reflections in use, adjusting your position so that you can see the majority of the room at all times. In confined spaces like elevators, trains, or public restrooms, it means avoiding blind corners and keeping your back to walls when possible. In vehicles, it means knowing how to exit quickly—not just through the front doors, but through windows or rear compartments if necessary. In stairwells or hallways, it means recognizing cover and concealment: where can you hide, where can you shield, and where can you run?

Environmental threat assessment is not paranoia—it is preparation. It is living with the awareness that if danger ever finds you, you will not be frozen. You will be ready, and you will already have mapped the terrain in your mind. Because while the attacker might control the time and place, they should *never* be the only one controlling the outcome.

1.3 The OODA Loop in Personal Combat

Once a potential threat has been identified, the clock starts ticking. In those next few seconds, the ability to process what is happening and act accordingly becomes the true test. This is where the OODA Loop becomes not just useful—but vital.

The OODA Loop—short for Observe, Orient, Decide, Act—was developed by U.S. Air Force Colonel John Boyd to explain how pilots make decisions under pressure. What he discovered is that whoever can complete this loop faster—not just once, but continuously—will dominate. The concept has since been adopted by everyone from fighter pilots to ground troops, law enforcement, and private security. And it applies to personal self-defense just as powerfully.

Let's start with observation. At first glance, this may seem synonymous with awareness, but in the context of the OODA Loop, it is more than just noticing. It is *active information gathering*—taking in details about your immediate environment, potential threats, obstacles, and opportunities. Special operations forces are trained to conduct this form of scanning even during chaotic moments. In an urban reconnaissance setting, for instance, a unit member may enter a room and in seconds register the number of people present, their body language, weapon potential, the location of exits, reflective surfaces, and barriers—all while keeping verbal situational dialogue with the team.

For civilians, observation doesn't require tactical gear. But it does require mental discipline. It means training yourself to look *through* the environment, not just at it. Are the people around you calm or tense? Are there areas of the room that feel off-limits or overly dark? Is there a person lingering too long without a purpose? Is there a group dynamic shifting—a sudden silence, a new arrival, a closed circle forming? These are signs that should trigger the second phase: orientation.

Orientation is the most misunderstood part of the loop, and yet it is where most people falter. It is the mental alignment of your perceptions with your internal models of reality. In other words, it's the act of interpreting what you've observed through the filters of training, experience, culture, emotional state, and available options. Two people might observe the same situation, but orient completely differently—one sees danger, the other sees a misunderstanding. The key to surviving violence is to train your orientation filter to favor action based on *patterns* rather than assumptions.

This means accounting for terrain. Are you near cover? On slippery ground? Are there civilians that could be endangered by your movement? Are there potential weapons within reach? It also means understanding legal boundaries. If you act too soon, you risk being the aggressor in the eyes of the law. If you act too late, you may be too injured—or dead—to worry about legality. This tension must be resolved in the orientation phase. And the only way to do that reliably is to run thousands of scenarios mentally, so that your interpretation becomes second nature.

Once you have oriented, you must decide. Decision is the point where hesitation either dies or wins. This is where most victims lose their chance. They second-guess themselves, weighing options for too long. The mind clogs with questions: Should I speak? Should I run? Should I strike? Should I yell? That indecision is precisely what the attacker is counting on. Every second you hesitate is a second you lose momentum—and a second they gain.

Combat-tested decision trees are tools that simplify this process. These are mental models that pre-determine your actions in specific situations, so you're not improvising under stress. For example, "If someone enters my home uninvited at night and I cannot retreat safely, I will use force to defend myself and my family." Or, "If I'm followed for more than two blocks and verbal engagement fails, I will change direction three times. If they still follow, I will enter a public space and call authorities."

Decisions made in advance, based on clear conditions, eliminate paralysis.

Finally comes action. This is the kinetic expression of everything you've processed. The key here is *speed with purpose*. It is not enough to act first—you must act *correctly*. Whether that's creating distance, executing a strike, drawing a weapon, or moving toward an exit, your action must be deliberate. Sloppy movement opens you up. Precise movement shuts the door on your opponent's plan.

The OODA Loop is not a one-time sequence. It's a feedback cycle. After you act, you must immediately begin observing again—has your action shifted the threat dynamic? Has the attacker changed posture, brought out a weapon, retreated, or escalated? You then re-orient, re-decide, re-act.

In combat, this loop happens in seconds, sometimes milliseconds. But with enough training, your loop becomes faster and sharper than your attacker's. That is the goal. To operate inside their decision cycle—so that while they are still thinking about their next move, you've already executed yours and are planning the next one.

And when you master that, *you* become the one with the advantage.

Chapter 2: The Warrior's Mindset

"I will either find a way or make one."
— Hannibal

2.1 Psychological Conditioning for Violence

Most people live under the comforting illusion that violence is something distant—reserved for movies, war zones, or unfortunate headlines involving someone else. But the truth is that violence is immediate, visceral, and far more common than we like to admit. It doesn't ask permission. It doesn't wait for you to be ready. When it arrives, it erupts suddenly, without warning, without rules.

And when it does, there are two kinds of people: those who freeze, and those who act.

This chapter is about becoming the second kind—not through bravado or fantasy, but through deliberate psychological reconditioning. We are not talking about becoming a violent person. We are talking about preparing the mind to engage in violence *when necessary*—as a tool of survival, as a last resort, as a means of protecting your own life or the lives of others. This mindset is not about cruelty. It's about clarity.

To engage in violence deliberately, efficiently, and morally under extreme stress requires a mental transformation that most civilians never undergo. The body cannot go where the mind has not already been. No matter how much training you've had in technique, if your mind is unprepared for the psychological toll of real violence, it will betray you. Your hands may know what to do, but your brain may lock you out at the worst possible moment.

That is why the first task in becoming truly dangerous—*in the right way*—is psychological conditioning.

Let's begin with what professionals call **stress inoculation**.

This process mirrors the way vaccines work. Just as small doses of a virus prepare the immune system to handle the real thing, controlled exposure to high-stress scenarios trains the mind and nervous system to operate under extreme pressure. Stress inoculation is not about teaching technique—it's about teaching resilience. The goal is to create familiarity with discomfort, so that when your heart races and your vision narrows, you do not panic. You recognize the signs, and you move forward anyway.

The human body under threat undergoes predictable changes. Adrenaline floods the bloodstream. Blood is redirected from the extremities toward the core. Fine motor skills degrade. Auditory exclusion kicks in. Time perception distorts. These physiological responses are ancient—they are hardwired survival mechanisms. But they are also potential liabilities if you've never experienced them before.

Stress inoculation training replicates these sensations in controlled environments. This might include sparring under fatigue, performing tactical drills after sprinting, engaging in simulated attacks while under time pressure, or training with unexpected loud noises, flashing lights, or disorienting instructions. The point is not to make you perfect—it is to make you *functional* under pressure. Because in real violence, perfection is a myth. The victor is not the person who moves flawlessly. It is the person who keeps moving when everyone else freezes.

But inoculation is only the beginning.

Once you've exposed yourself to high-stress environments, you must then learn to compartmentalize.

Compartmentalization is a psychological defense mechanism often used by military special forces, trauma surgeons, hostage negotiators, and others who operate regularly in environments where death and suffering are unavoidable. It is the ability to temporarily suspend emotional processing in order to maintain operational focus. It does not mean suppressing emotion. It means delaying it. You do what needs to be done now. You deal with how it made you feel later.

In the context of violence, this skill becomes crucial. When you are forced to defend yourself—or someone you love—against a real, immediate threat, you may be exposed to blood, screaming, broken bones, even the death of your attacker. If your psyche is not prepared for that, you may hesitate, or worse, shut down entirely. Your civilized conditioning will scream: *This is wrong. This is chaos. This cannot be real.*

Compartmentalization allows you to silence that scream—not permanently, but long enough to survive.

Veterans of real-world violence often speak of entering a different space during combat—an altered state where time slows, decisions become mechanical, and emotions feel distant. This is not a dissociative disorder. This is trained focus. The ability to put horror in a box, lock the box, and keep functioning. Later, in safety, that box must be opened. Emotions must be processed. Otherwise, trauma will take root. But in the moment? Emotion is a luxury you can't afford.

To train this skill, you must practice operating under emotional stress. This doesn't mean inducing trauma. It means simulating difficult moral or ethical scenarios and making decisions within them. It means mental rehearsal, visualization, and real-time scenario work that challenges not just your body, but your values. Would you strike someone pointing a gun at your child? Would you break a limb to stop an attacker choking your partner? Would you keep fighting after being stabbed?

These are not pleasant thoughts. But they are necessary ones. Because when that moment comes, you do not want to be making these decisions for the first time.

Which brings us to the final piece of this section: the **survival switch**.

Every human being carries within them a mechanism—a deeply buried neurological trigger—that can override years of social programming in an instant. This is the survival switch. It is the point at which your body and mind agree that violence is not only justified, but required. That you will do *whatever it takes* to live.

For many, this switch is never accessed. For others, it activates too late. For some, it's blocked entirely by the lifelong internal command: *Do no harm.* While this command is noble, it can be fatal in the wrong context.

The key is to understand that morality and survival are not enemies. The survival switch is not about becoming a monster. It is about becoming the kind of person who is willing to be terrifying—for exactly as long as is necessary—to protect something greater than themselves.

To train this reflex, you must change your identity.

Not in the philosophical sense, but in the biological one. The brain works on identity loops. If you see yourself as a gentle person, a peaceful person, a non-confrontational person—those traits, while admirable, may interfere when violence is the only path forward. The answer is not to discard that identity. It is to *expand it*. You must come to believe that you are both. That you are kind *and* capable of ferocity. That you are calm *and* unstoppable when cornered. That your peace is not weakness, but control.

Training the survival switch means building permission into your nervous system. You must teach your body that there is a time when unleashing your full power is not only allowed, but required. You must visualize this. Feel it. Rehearse it mentally, physically, emotionally. Only then will your system recognize the moment when that permission must become action.

The switch is not activated by rage. It is activated by *clarity*. The clarity that no one is coming to save you. That your life depends on your willingness to commit, fully and without hesitation, to the fight at hand. That there are no referees, no do-overs, no safe words.

In that moment, you do not rise to the occasion. You fall back on your training. And if that training has included stress inoculation, compartmentalization, and survival conditioning, you will act with power, precision, and moral confidence.

Without these tools, your instinct may betray you. You may freeze. You may fight half-heartedly. You may allow the fear of harming someone else to override the reality that they are actively trying to harm *you*.

Violence is ugly. But sometimes, it is necessary. And when that time comes, hesitation is not mercy—it is surrender. The Warrior's Mindset is not about embracing violence. It is about mastering it. About ensuring that if you are ever forced to step into that arena, you will do so prepared—physically, yes, but more importantly, mentally.

Because the mind *is* the battlefield.

And those who train it win before the fight begins.

2.2 Managing Fear and Adrenaline

No matter how well-trained or experienced someone may be, fear is a biological certainty in the presence of real danger. The moment you recognize a situation as life-threatening—whether it's the sudden closing of distance by an aggressive individual, the unmistakable metallic glint of a weapon, or simply the eerie intuition that something is about to go wrong—your body responds instantly. Adrenaline surges. Your heart rate spikes. Blood leaves your extremities and pools in your core. Your vision may narrow. Your hearing may become distorted. Your muscles tense, ready to explode into motion—or lock into paralysis.

This reaction is ancient. It was forged long before language, in the caves and savannahs where our ancestors either fought or fled. It is the survival system firing at full power. But while it can help you survive, it can also cause you to freeze, to flail, or to miscalculate in the moments that matter most. That is why understanding how to manage fear and adrenaline is as important as any physical technique.

The first lever of control in this storm of chemical activity is the breath. Breathing is the only aspect of the autonomic nervous system that we can consciously influence in real-time. Through breath, we regain control over heart rate, oxygen delivery to the brain, and ultimately, our decision-making capacity. In combat training, this is known as tactical breathing or combat breathing.

Tactical breathing involves slow, deliberate respiratory cycles—usually four seconds in, four seconds hold, four seconds out, and four seconds hold again. This technique does not eliminate fear, but it regulates the physiological symptoms of panic. When practiced regularly, it allows individuals to slow their heart rate, maintain fine motor skills, and keep their minds from becoming overwhelmed. It is the anchor in chaos.

Military units, law enforcement officers, and elite athletes use this type of breathing not just to calm down, but to shift mental states—from reactive to responsive, from frantic to focused. In moments of intense threat, when every second counts, a single controlled breath can prevent an impulsive mistake and restore composure. That breath buys time—and time buys life.

But sometimes, fear takes hold faster than breath control can respond. This is where the freeze response becomes relevant.

Freezing is not weakness. It is not cowardice. It is a deeply ingrained survival reflex—a third option in the fight-or-flight model that is often ignored. The freeze response is the body's way of assessing overwhelming danger by pausing all action. In the wild, freezing can save an animal's life. Stillness avoids detection. Delay allows a more accurate read of the threat.

But in human conflict—particularly close-quarters violence—freezing can be deadly. You cannot allow yourself to remain locked in that state when an attacker closes distance or launches a strike. Therefore, training must address not just how to fight or flee, but how to *unfreeze*.

The most effective method of overriding the freeze response is *preloaded motion*. This means training your body to initiate a simple, aggressive physical response the moment it detects certain danger cues. For instance, a forward step with hands up in a defensive frame. A sudden verbal command. A default striking motion. The point is not to execute a perfect technique, but to *break inertia*. Once motion begins, the nervous system often follows.

This override mechanism is built through repetition. Drills that simulate sudden attacks—especially from unexpected directions—train the body to move immediately, even before conscious thought completes. The moment an individual begins to move, even slightly, the freeze dissipates. Adrenaline is redirected toward action. Muscle memory takes over. And with motion comes momentum.

In conjunction with unfreezing, the warrior must learn to harness the power of aggression—not rage, not blind fury, but *channeled aggression*. When fear floods the system, it can paralyze. But when it is redirected, it becomes fuel. The key is not to suppress fear, but to let it trigger controlled violence.

Channeling aggression involves mental conditioning and physical outlets. In training, this might look like explosive drills, impact training with pads or bags, or scenario-based sparring with verbal engagement. But more importantly, it requires internal permission. You must accept the fact that, when threatened, it is not only okay—it is necessary—to become a force of destruction for a brief, deliberate moment.

The mistake many make is believing that aggression and awareness are mutually exclusive. They are not. The most effective fighters are those who can flip the aggression switch without losing tactical clarity. They strike with purpose, not emotion. They move with speed, not recklessness. Their aggression is directed, precise, and underpinned by a clear goal: neutralize the threat and regain control of the environment.

Fear and adrenaline will never go away. Nor should they. They are part of your natural arsenal. But they must be mastered. A fearful person who controls their body becomes dangerous. A panicked person who can breathe, move, and act becomes unpredictable. And unpredictability—when combined with training—is a weapon all its own.

2.3 Mental Rehearsal and Scenario Planning

Preparation for violence does not end with the body. In truth, the most powerful preparation happens inside the mind. Because before you ever engage in a real-world confrontation, your brain must have visited that terrain—felt its weight, seen its rhythm, understood its consequences. This is the power of mental rehearsal.

Visualization is not just a motivational tactic. It is a neurophysiological tool with measurable impact. When you imagine performing a task—whether it's lifting a weight, executing a technique, or navigating a violent encounter—your brain activates the same neural pathways as it would during the actual event. In essence, your body begins to learn even in stillness. Elite performers in every field—from special forces operators to professional athletes—use visualization to prime their nervous systems for performance under pressure.

In combat training, visualization should be detailed, multi-sensory, and situational. You don't just imagine "fighting." You imagine the environment. The lighting. The sounds. The emotions. The attacker's face. The timing of your movements. You run the scenario like a film—pausing, rewinding, changing the outcome. You feel fear, then override it. You make a mistake, then correct it. Over time, your brain stores these rehearsals as *experience*. When the real thing occurs, you won't be starting from zero.

To maximize the impact of visualization, you must rehearse *specific situations*. This leads to what is called "if-then conditioning." This is the mental equivalent of pre-programmed responses. It means building a library of scenarios in your mind and attaching clear, decisive actions to each.

If someone blocks your path and begins shouting obscenities, then you create distance, raise your hands, and speak with authority. If someone grabs your wrist near a vehicle, then you twist out and strike the closest available target. If you're cornered in an alley, then you identify cover, look for escape paths, and prepare to engage.

These conditionals allow your brain to skip the paralysis of uncertainty. When the mind is under stress, decision-making slows. The more complex the situation, the greater the cognitive load. But if you've already made the decision in training, your response becomes reflexive. This doesn't guarantee a perfect outcome. But it gives you a starting point—and in violence, starting fast often means staying alive.

Beyond the immediate confrontation, mental preparation must also address what happens *after* the fight.

Too often, self-defense training ends with the physical victory. But in reality, survival is followed by consequences—legal, emotional, social. If you have seriously injured or killed someone in defense of your life, you will not walk away unaffected. The body may be intact, but the mind will carry echoes.

This is why post-incident mental frameworks are critical. You must prepare yourself for what comes next—not just practically, but morally. After the adrenaline fades, you may feel guilt, shame, or confusion. You may second-guess your decisions. Others may question you, or even blame you. You must be ready to hold your ground.

R.A.T. Fight

This begins with truth: If you acted lawfully, ethically, and as a last resort, then your actions were justified. That clarity must be embedded before the event, not rationalized after. In your mental rehearsal, you must walk through the aftermath. The arrival of police. The questioning. The statements. The looks from onlookers. The calls from family members. You must rehearse speaking clearly. Telling the truth. Asking for counsel. Repeating, if necessary, that you feared for your life and acted in defense of yourself or others.

Processing the emotional weight is another task. You may need time. You may need support. You may need silence. But you must also be honest with yourself: Violence was chosen *for you*. You responded not with malice, but with necessity. This distinction matters. It is the line between becoming hardened and becoming haunted.

And finally, scenario planning must include debrief and reflection. After any training scenario—real or imagined—ask yourself: What worked? What didn't? What will I do differently next time? This habit sharpens the mind. It builds humility and adaptability. It ensures that every experience, even the mental ones, becomes a stepping stone toward greater readiness.

In the end, preparation is not paranoia. It is responsibility. It is the quiet acknowledgment that while you cannot control when violence arrives, you *can* control your response to it.

You will never eliminate fear. You will never fully prevent adrenaline. But you can train them, ride them, and bend them to your will. And when you do, you become more than a survivor.

You become a weapon in defense of life.

Chapter 3: Biomechanics of Destruction

> *"The best technique is the one that works when you need it most."*
> — Tim Larkin

3.1 Human Anatomy as a Weapon System

Violence is not about elegance. It's not about style, form, or choreography. In real-life self-defense, the goal is not to look good but to stop the threat—decisively, immediately, and without hesitation. When life is on the line, there are no points for grace. What matters is *effectiveness*. And the most effective way to neutralize a threat is to understand how to use the human body—both your own and your attacker's—as a weapon system.

The body is not built for combat. It's built for survival, yes—but not to take damage. The human machine, despite its remarkable endurance and complexity, is fragile in certain areas. It's full of structural weaknesses, vulnerable clusters, and pressure points that can be exploited with surprising efficiency. And when your life is under threat, knowing exactly where to strike—and how to do so with maximum impact—can tilt the odds dramatically in your favor, even if your opponent is stronger, faster, or armed.

Let's begin with the concept of high-value targets. These are areas of the body that, when attacked correctly, produce disproportionately powerful results. The eyes, throat, groin, knees, and certain nerve clusters are not protected by muscle or bone in the same way that other parts of the body are. They are poorly defended, highly sensitive, and essential to the attacker's ability to function.

The eyes, for instance, are among the most psychologically and physically disabling targets available. A single gouge, rake, or thrust to the ocular cavity can cause a temporary or permanent loss of vision, disorientation, and panic. It doesn't require strength—it requires intent. The fear of eye damage alone is often enough to make an attacker recoil. But in a life-or-death struggle, hesitation must be cast aside. You are not fighting to win a match. You are fighting to remain alive. And in that context, the eyes are fair game.

The throat is another critical point. It sits unguarded at the front of the neck, vulnerable to crushing, choking, or tearing pressure. A strike to the trachea disrupts breathing and can induce gagging, panic, or collapse. Even light force applied to the carotid arteries on either side of the neck can reduce blood flow to the brain, creating disorientation or unconsciousness within seconds. For those trained in this kind of targeting, the neck becomes not a vague region but a map of opportunity—where the trachea, larynx, arteries, and vertebrae each represent different levels of tactical leverage.

The groin, often mocked in popular culture as a cheap shot, is in fact one of the most accessible and devastating targets in a fight. Not just for men—though the testicles are clearly vulnerable—but for women as well. The perineum and pelvic nerves are sensitive, easily shocked, and capable of shutting down motor function when struck with proper force. Kicks, knees, or upward strikes delivered with speed and commitment can instantly disrupt the attacker's structure and rhythm.

Beyond these soft targets, we must look at the skeletal system—particularly the joints. Joints are the hinges of movement. Disrupt them, and the attacker cannot pursue, grab, or strike effectively. The knees and elbows are particularly susceptible to breaks, hyperextension, and dislocation. A well-timed lateral kick to the side of a knee can end a confrontation in less than a second, collapsing the attacker's base and rendering their weight-bearing leg useless. The shoulder joint, with its wide range of motion and relatively shallow socket, is also vulnerable to wrenching motions that separate it from its structural alignment.

But even more valuable than targeting these areas is the understanding of *how* to hit them. This is where biomechanics come in. Power in a strike doesn't come from the arms or legs alone—it comes from the entire body, moving as a unified system. Too many people assume that physical strength determines who wins a fight. In reality, technique and body mechanics often trump brute force.

Force multiplication is the key to making your strikes count, especially against a larger or stronger opponent. It's not about fighting harder. It's about fighting *smarter*. When you align your hips, shoulders, and spine with the direction of your strike, when you generate torque through rotation and follow-through, you produce exponentially more power than isolated limb movement ever could. It's the difference between throwing a punch with your arm and driving it with your entire frame. The first may sting. The second can break bones.

This principle applies to every kind of strike—punches, elbows, knees, and kicks. It also applies to grappling. Leverage, not strength, is what allows a smaller person to break a larger person's joint or choke them unconscious. By manipulating angles, isolating limbs, and applying pressure at the right point of the joint, you override the attacker's physical advantage. That's why understanding body mechanics is not optional—it is essential.

When force is generated correctly, the attacker feels not just pain, but systemic failure. Their body doesn't just hurt—it stops working. That's the goal. You're not trying to "win" a fight. You're trying to *end* it—suddenly, violently, and with no ambiguity. This is not cruelty. It is necessity. The longer a violent encounter lasts, the greater your risk. Your goal is not endurance. It is *resolution*.

Now let's examine how everyday objects can enter this equation.

In real-world violence, you rarely have the luxury of being armed in a conventional sense. You may not be carrying a knife, a baton, or even pepper spray. But the world around you is full of tools—if you know how to use them.

Weapon integration is the practice of taking ordinary objects and turning them into force multipliers. A pen becomes a dagger. A flashlight becomes a bludgeon. A key becomes a gouging tool. A belt becomes a whip or a garrote. The object doesn't matter nearly as much as the *intent* behind its use and the targeting of its application. The best improvised weapons are those that are immediately accessible, require no preparation, and can be employed without alerting the attacker in advance.

For example, a rolled-up magazine, when gripped tightly, becomes a makeshift baton capable of striking with surprising force. A ceramic coffee mug, smashed against an edge, becomes a jagged edge weapon. A metal water bottle can knock someone unconscious with a single strike if delivered to the temple or jawline. These are not theories. These are documented cases. And they are reminders that weapons are everywhere—you simply have to recognize them as such.

What matters most in weapon integration is *speed of employment*. You must be able to identify, access, and deploy the object in seconds. This requires environmental awareness. You must constantly scan your surroundings—not just for threats, but for resources. When you enter a room, ask yourself: What can I use if things go sideways? Where is the nearest object with weight, rigidity, or edge? Where can I move to gain access to tools others might ignore?

Training with improvised weapons helps bridge the gap between theory and instinct. You begin to see the world not as a neutral environment, but as an arsenal of potential advantages. Your attacker may come armed—but if you've trained your mind and body to adapt, you will not be outmatched for long.

Ultimately, turning the body into a weapon system is about removing hesitation. You must stop seeing violence as a contest of strength or a test of skill. It is neither. It is a problem to be solved with finality and decisiveness. The human body—your own and your opponent's—is the medium through which that problem is addressed.

When you understand anatomical vulnerabilities, when you move with biomechanical precision, and when you leverage the objects around you to amplify your force, you become something more than just a person who knows how to fight. You become an entity that finishes fights.

The biomechanical principles of destruction are not abstract. They are tactile, functional, and brutally efficient. And when combined with the right mindset, they allow even the smallest individual to stop a much larger threat—without needing luck, without relying on help, and without wasting time.

3.2 Efficient Movement Under Stress

In a life-threatening encounter, adrenaline doesn't just rush through the body—it commandeers it. Under stress, the body simplifies. Fine motor control deteriorates. Vision narrows. The hands shake. What once felt like a basic motion in the gym or dojo becomes an impossible tangle when your heart is pounding and your brain is screaming for survival. This is not a malfunction. It's biology doing its job—diverting energy to large muscle groups, preparing you to run or fight, often at the cost of precision.

The mistake many make in self-defense training is overinvesting in complex techniques that require calm, step-by-step execution. Reality doesn't grant you that luxury. Your opponent won't wait for you to recall the third step of a wristlock or the angle of a fancy disarm. Under duress, you fall back to what your body can do automatically—and what it *can do well* without fine motor precision.

That's why gross motor skill prioritization matters.

Gross motor skills involve large, powerful movements—palm strikes, elbows, knee drives, shoulder checks, kicks, full-body throws. These movements are not only easier to retain under stress, they also deliver more force and are more adaptable across a wider range of body types and situations. You don't need perfect form to drive a knee into an attacker's groin. You don't need months of training to shove someone backward with your entire body weight. But you *do* need the instinct to use these movements without hesitation, and the experience to do so with balance and intention.

This brings us to the concept of *economy of motion*.

In combat, every unnecessary movement is a liability. The more you flail, overextend, or exaggerate your strikes, the more energy you burn, the more openings you create for your opponent, and the more control you lose over your own body. Efficiency is not about moving fast—it's about eliminating wasted effort. The shortest path from your shoulder to your target is a straight line.

The most effective footwork isn't the flashiest—it's the one that keeps you mobile while preserving balance and power.

Economy of motion doesn't mean fighting passively. It means fighting smart. It means training your body to generate maximum force with minimal movement. A short, tight elbow thrown from close range can do more damage than a wild overhand punch if your core, hips, and posture are aligned. A subtle shift in foot position can let you rotate into a strike with full-body torque, even in a crowded space.

The more efficient your motion, the longer you can sustain intensity in a fight. Most violent encounters are over in seconds, but if you're not trained to conserve energy and strike with intent, those seconds may feel like an eternity. Especially if you're outnumbered or outmatched, efficiency becomes the great equalizer. You don't want to be the fastest or the strongest—you want to be the *least wasteful*.

That brings us to balance and positioning, perhaps the most underappreciated elements of real-world combat.

Without balance, you cannot generate power. Without positioning, you cannot deliver force where it matters. Many people assume that staying on their feet is about avoiding takedowns—but it's more than that. Staying upright gives you visibility, mobility, and dominance over space. Once you lose your footing, you're no longer fighting on your terms. You're surviving.

Balance is not static. It is dynamic—a fluid dance between rootedness and movement. Good fighters don't just stand firm; they move through chaos with poise. They know how to plant a foot without locking a knee. They know when to shift weight forward to drive an elbow and when to lean back to absorb a push. In unstable environments—a wet floor, a sloped alley, a cramped hallway—this control of balance becomes critical. You're not just fighting your attacker. You're fighting gravity, terrain, and unpredictability.

Positioning is about where you are in relation to your opponent. Are you inside their range or just outside it? Are you centered or offset? Do you have access to their weak side? Are you angling your body to reduce the target area? A good position allows you to strike without getting hit. A great position allows you to dominate without overcommitting. It keeps your options open—for attack, for defense, for escape.

Efficient movement under stress is not a natural gift. It is built through repetition, through realistic scenarios, through physical fatigue and mental pressure. You must learn how to move when your breath is short, your hands are shaking, and your muscles are flooded with lactic acid. Only then will your movement become not just survival—but strategy.

3.3 Timing and Distance Management

In every violent encounter, there exists a critical space—a gap between safety and danger, between readiness and reaction. This is known as the *reactionary gap*, and it defines the time and distance necessary to recognize a threat, make a decision, and respond effectively before the attacker can land a decisive blow. Most people underestimate this space. They assume that if someone is three or four feet away, they'll have time to react. But in reality, a motivated attacker can close that distance in less than a second.

That second is your window. Your entire survival may hinge on how you manage it.

Managing the reactionary gap is not just about distance—it's about awareness. If you are unaware, your gap is much larger. You might need three or four seconds to respond because you're not even registering the threat. If you are alert, your gap shrinks. You see the signs before movement begins. You anticipate the draw of a weapon, the sudden shift in posture, the clenching of fists. And because you see it early, you can act early.

Distance is relative. A man twenty feet away with a gun is more dangerous than a man five feet away with a knife—depending on where you're standing, what cover exists, and what your environment allows. Understanding this shifting relationship is part of what separates a survivor from a victim. You must constantly reevaluate space—not as emptiness, but as opportunity. Space to move, space to strike, space to escape.

When you recognize that the attacker is within range and escalation is imminent, *entry* becomes the next strategic move.

Entry techniques, borrowed from military close-quarters combat, are designed to close the gap without absorbing the full force of an incoming attack. This might involve shifting off the centerline, angling your body to redirect force, or crashing in to smother the attacker's momentum. The purpose of a good entry is to deny your opponent space. When you control the entry, you dictate the terms of engagement.

Many civilians instinctively backpedal during a confrontation, believing that distance equals safety. But without training, backing up often leads to losing balance, tripping, or being cornered. Controlled forward movement—initiated at the right time—can be far more effective. A well-timed step inside a punch not only neutralizes its power, it also puts you in a dominant position to strike, trap, or take down.

R.A.T. Fight

In multiple attacker scenarios, entries become even more important. You must create angles that isolate one opponent from the others, breaking up their formation. If you stand in the middle, you get flanked. If you move aggressively to the outside and disrupt their spacing, you force them to adjust—and in that adjustment, you find your openings.

However, not every fight should be finished. There is a moment in every encounter when the goal shifts from domination to escape. You've stunned the attacker. You've created separation. Now you must disengage.

Disengagement protocols are not about walking away casually. They are about transitioning from offense to exit *without* becoming vulnerable. This often involves delivering a final, decisive strike—a knee, an elbow, a shove—to create a window. Then, using that moment, you move swiftly and deliberately to safety. You do not wait to see if they're getting up. You do not argue. You get out.

The direction of disengagement matters. Running toward your car, your home, or even a crowd can be smart—but only if those routes are safe and clear. The terrain must be factored in. Are you running into a dead end? Are you exposing your back in a narrow hallway? Are you placing yourself between the attacker and their accomplices?

You must train to disengage with the same precision you train to strike. Practice break-contact drills. Practice scanning for exit routes *before* a threat begins. Practice shifting from aggression to movement, from fighting to fleeing—not because you're losing, but because the fight is over.

And if escape is not possible, your timing must shift again. You return to offense, but now with urgency. Every movement becomes either an attempt to regain mobility or to end the threat permanently. There is no middle ground.

Timing and distance are not abstract concepts. They are the bedrock of tactical self-defense. If you strike too early, you may miss. Too late, and you're already hit. If you move too close, you get tied up. Too far, and you lose control. The sweet spot changes with every second. Your job is to find it faster than your opponent does.

Training for this kind of decision-making is not theoretical. It's built in sparring, in scenario drills, in controlled chaos. You learn how to read the micro-movements that signal attack. You learn how to time your entry like a predator. You learn how to feel when it's time to break off—not because you're afraid, but because you've already won.

A fight is not just about who hits harder. It's about who moves better, who sees more, who chooses the right moment to act—and the right moment to stop. In that space between motion and stillness lies survival.

Chapter 4: Close Quarters Combat Systems

"Get in close, hit hard, get out fast."
— British SAS Motto

4.1 Empty Hand Combat Techniques

Fighting at a distance is a luxury that most real-world encounters don't afford. When violence happens suddenly, it often does so in tight spaces—elevators, hallways, cars, stairwells, kitchens, bathrooms—places where footwork is limited, range disappears, and control becomes a matter of inches, not feet. This is the domain of close quarters combat, where every strike must be deliberate, every motion efficient, and hesitation is not just costly—it's fatal.

At these ranges, traditional boxing-style punches often lose their effectiveness. The mechanics of a full jab or cross require space to generate torque and speed. But in a confined environment, with a threat just inches away, the body needs to shift to tools designed for proximity, impact, and durability. Empty hand combat techniques are the backbone of such engagement, and the most effective tools are those that rely on gross motor patterns, dense contact surfaces, and instinctive mechanics that remain accessible under extreme pressure.

Among the most reliable tools in this setting is the hammer fist. Unlike a traditional punch, which utilizes the fragile knuckles of the clenched fist, the hammer fist relies on the thick, bony underside of the hand—the side opposite the thumb—delivering a blunt-force strike that carries minimal risk of self-injury. This makes it ideal for striking hard targets like the face, clavicle, or ribs without compromising your own hand structure.

The beauty of the hammer fist lies in its simplicity. The motion mimics that of swinging a tool or slamming a heavy object downward. It's familiar, even to the untrained. Whether thrown from high to low, across the centerline, or diagonally from the shoulder, the hammer fist allows you to generate serious impact using the body's natural rotation. It's also highly adaptable. You can use it standing, kneeling, or on the ground. From clinch range or in a scramble, the hammer fist can rain down repeatedly without the need for complex setups.

In chaotic situations where fine motor control collapses and adrenaline floods the system, the hammer fist's reliability stands out. It is structurally sound, instinctively accessible, and delivers percussive force that can disorient, break posture, and open up follow-up options. A well-placed hammer fist to the nose or ear can stagger an attacker, while a barrage to the collarbone or jaw can collapse their posture entirely.

But hammer fists, while powerful, are not the only weapons designed for tight quarters. The body comes equipped with even more devastating tools, especially when there's no room to throw traditional punches. Elbows and knees are the evolutionary sledgehammers of the human frame—dense, bone-heavy joints that deliver force through short, brutal arcs.

The elbow is one of the most lethal weapons in close quarters. It requires almost no space to deploy and can be thrown from nearly any angle—horizontal, vertical, downward, upward, spinning. The force it delivers is concentrated over a small surface area, which amplifies its impact. In a confined hallway or during a clinch, elbows can be the deciding factor. A sharp elbow to the orbital socket can break bone, cause immediate disorientation, or even knock someone unconscious. The compact nature of the movement also makes it hard to detect and even harder to block.

Equally important is the knee. In close proximity, especially when an attacker is trying to grapple or control you, the knee can strike upward into the groin, downward into the thigh, or forward into the ribs, solar plexus, or head. The vertical path of a rising knee strike is perfect for disrupting the attacker's centerline, damaging internal structures, or creating distance. If the opponent is hunched forward, whether from a clinch or after absorbing a body shot, the knee becomes a natural follow-up.

Elbows and knees are brutal in their application but elegant in their function. They bypass the need for range, require minimal wind-up, and allow the defender to stay compact and protected while delivering damage. More importantly, they function well under stress. They don't require precision to be effective—only intent and momentum. A slightly misaligned elbow is still devastating. A knee that lands off-center still disrupts the attacker's structure.

Training these tools should involve repetition under resistance, so they become part of the defender's instinctive reaction set. Pad work, clinch drills, and scenario-based training build the confidence to use these strikes when confined, grabbed, or slammed against a wall. When combined with solid foot positioning and hip control, the elbow and knee become reliable weapons in virtually any close-range environment.

And then there's the fine work—the precision strikes that target soft tissues, nerves, and vulnerable sensory areas. While gross motor tools like hammer fists and elbows deliver power, thumb and finger attacks offer *opportunity*. They don't rely on strength. They rely on accuracy and audacity.

The eyes are a universal equalizer. There is no training, no conditioning, no level of strength that allows a person to resist an intentional eye gouge or rake. The body will respond instantly to a threat to vision. A finger jab to the eye causes immediate pain, involuntary flinching, and momentary blindness—enough to disrupt the attack and allow follow-up or escape. Even the threat of eye contact can be enough to cause an attacker to hesitate. In an ambush scenario or during a ground struggle, the ability to target the eyes with thumbs or fingers can neutralize an otherwise overwhelming threat.

Likewise, the throat remains an extremely vulnerable target. A thumb driven into the soft tissue just above the collarbone can cause a gag reflex, disrupt breathing, or collapse the trachea with enough force. In tight quarters, a hand to the throat—whether pushing, grabbing, or striking—can radically alter the balance of control. It doesn't require strength. It requires placement and intent.

Nerve points, while often exaggerated in martial arts lore, are nonetheless valid when targeted correctly. The brachial plexus, located on the side of the neck beneath the ear, is particularly sensitive. A thumb pressed into this area during a clinch can create a shock-like effect, weakening the opponent's arm or causing involuntary movement. The radial nerve, located near the forearm just below the elbow, can also be disrupted with a sharp strike, causing temporary paralysis or loss of grip.

Thumb and finger attacks are not about finesse—they are about *interruption*. In a violent encounter, your goal is not to overpower your attacker—it is to disrupt their ability to continue attacking. A single jab to the eye, a press to the windpipe, a thumb in a nerve cluster—these moments break rhythm, cause panic, and create opening. You don't need to end the fight with a finger strike. You need it to open the door for something that will.

Training these techniques requires caution and control. Because of their potential for injury, they should be practiced with partners in a cooperative manner before being drilled under pressure. The goal is to make them familiar—not to simulate injury, but to encode movement pathways that can be accessed when needed. Once those pathways are wired, you won't need to think. The hand will move on its own.

All empty hand techniques must be framed within a larger principle: decisiveness. The mistake that gets most people hurt in a close-quarters situation isn't lack of technique—it's hesitation. It's waiting for confirmation that the threat is real. It's hoping that the attacker will back down. But hope is not a strategy. When the moment arrives, you must strike first, strike hard, and keep striking until the threat no longer exists. That's not aggression—it's survival.

Hammer fists, elbows, knees, thumbs—they are not elegant. They are not pretty. But they work. They work when the lights are low, when the space is tight, when your heart is pounding and your brain is barely hanging on. They work when nothing else will. And that's why they matter.

Close quarters combat is the proving ground of real-world self-defense. There is no distance to create safety. There is no room to run. There is only you, your body, your will, and what you've trained it to do. When space disappears, everything must tighten—your movement, your breathing, your intent. There's no time to think. There's only time to *do*.

And what you do, when every second counts, will depend entirely on whether you've trained your empty hand tools to operate under fire.

4.2 Grappling and Ground Fighting

When violence breaks the plane of personal space and collapses into the clinch, the fight becomes a matter of control. This is where grappling begins—not as a sport, but as survival. At this range, the lines blur between striking, movement, and manipulation. You are not just trying to hurt the opponent—you're trying to deny them structure, space, and decision-making ability. In a street context, grappling isn't about scoring points or dominating for extended periods. It's about establishing vertical dominance, escaping dangerous positions quickly, and, if necessary, disabling the attacker with brutal precision.

The first principle in any real-world grappling situation is to maintain your feet. The moment you're taken to the ground, your options narrow drastically. You lose visibility, mobility, and access to escape. On the ground, you become vulnerable to stomps, head trauma against hard surfaces, and the worst-case scenario: a second attacker entering the scene. That's why standing grappling is not just a preference—it's a strategic imperative.

Maintaining vertical dominance requires a blend of balance, frame management, and timing. When someone attempts to grab, clinch, or drag you off your feet, your first task is to create structure within the chaos. This is done by establishing strong frames with your arms and elbows, using your hips to deny inward pressure, and keeping your base wide and staggered. If they shoot for a takedown, your sprawl must be immediate and violent—your hips driving downward, your forearms pushing against their shoulders, your legs anchoring to deny momentum.

But defensive grappling isn't passive. Once you've stopped the initial advance, you must take control. That could mean turning the clinch into a striking platform—elbows, knees, headbutts—or off-balancing them with foot sweeps, hip tosses, or sudden directional changes. A strong underhook can act like a lever, turning their torso and exposing their back. A collar tie can become a handle to drive their head downward into your knee. The key is to prevent entanglement. You're not trying to wrestle—you're trying to end the engagement or escape it. Every second you spend in the clinch is a gamble. End it before your opponent resets.

If, despite your best efforts, you go to the ground, the nature of the fight changes drastically. On your back, gravity works against you. Your field of vision is limited. If weapons are involved, your ability to detect or control them is compromised. And if there's more than one attacker, you're in serious danger. This is why modern military combatives and real-world self-defense systems train to treat the ground as a temporary problem, not a battlefield. The goal isn't to dominate—it's to escape.

Ground escape priorities are simple: protect vital areas, create space, and get up. Immediately. You don't have time to work for a triangle choke or attempt a slow, technical armbar. Your priority is to avoid strikes, manage posture, and create a wedge of space using your feet, hips, or elbows. Once you've made distance, you initiate a technical stand-up or explosive get-up, depending on the urgency. This means bracing on one hand, framing with the opposite foot, and rising while maintaining a protective posture. You never turn your back blindly. You never rise into a strike. The movement must be clean, controlled, and committed.

There are, of course, moments when ground control must turn into offense. If escape is not immediately possible, or if the attacker is already compromised, submission becomes a viable tool—not for points, but for resolution. And in real violence, submission is not a negotiation. It is damage.

Chokes and joint destruction techniques function because the human body cannot resist them for long. A properly applied blood choke, cutting off circulation to the brain through pressure on the carotid arteries, can cause unconsciousness in under ten seconds. This is not theoretical. It's been tested in combat, law enforcement, and countless real-world altercations. A rear naked choke, a guillotine, or a triangle can all accomplish this if locked correctly and held without interruption. The goal is not to wait for a tap—it's to neutralize the threat and immediately disengage.

Joint destruction techniques, meanwhile, focus on exploiting mechanical weaknesses in the elbows, shoulders, wrists, or knees. A standing kimura grip, if applied with a sudden torque, can dislocate the shoulder. An armbar applied with bodyweight—not finesse—can hyperextend the elbow and remove one limb from the fight. These techniques are dangerous by design. They do not require extended grappling exchanges. They are meant to be fast, final, and followed by escape.

The mindset in real grappling is simple: control only long enough to create the opening you need to escape or end the fight. Anything longer invites unpredictability, secondary attackers, or weapon threats. Whether you're dealing with a street brawl or a mugging in a narrow hallway, the same principles apply. Stay on your feet if you can. Get up immediately if you can't. And when you have to finish it on the ground, do so with certainty and violence—not hesitation.

4.3 Weapon Retention and Disarmament

The introduction of a weapon into a close-quarters confrontation changes the dynamics instantly. A fistfight becomes a potentially lethal encounter the moment steel, lead, or a blade is involved. But even more dangerous than an armed attacker is the moment when *you* are armed, and the attacker attempts to take your weapon. In that instant, the weapon becomes a liability as much as an asset. This is why weapon retention and disarmament are not optional skills—they are survival mandates.

Let's begin with firearm retention. Carrying a firearm in public, whether concealed or open, does not automatically make you safer. It makes you responsible. A gun is a tool of last resort, and if it is taken from you, the consequences are often fatal. In a physical struggle, especially when distance has collapsed, maintaining control of your firearm becomes priority number one.

Retention techniques are rooted in structure, not just grip strength. Your holster position, your body posture, your awareness of line of access—all of these determine whether the weapon remains yours in a fight. If someone goes for your gun, your first action isn't to pull back—it's to *trap* their hand against the weapon and drive your bodyweight into them. The goal is to eliminate the space that allows them to draw. You must turn into them, rotate your hips, control the wrist or forearm, and redirect the fight. Movement is essential. Standing still gets you overpowered. You must fight for angle, for leverage, and for superior positioning—because if they get control of the weapon's grip, your life is now in their hands.

This is why law enforcement officers train relentlessly on weapon retention in confined spaces. They don't rely on brute strength. They rely on posture, grip, movement, and explosive counters to redirect the weapon and retake initiative. You must do the same.

Now consider the reverse—disarming an attacker wielding a firearm at close range. Movies make this look easy. It's not. It is possible, but only under specific conditions: surprise, proximity, timing, and total commitment. A gun pointed at you from ten feet away is not disarmable without suicidal odds. A gun pressed to your chest, however, may present an opportunity.

Disarmament is not about grabbing the gun. It's about *redirecting* it—off the centerline, away from your vital organs—and immediately closing the distance to deny them use of the trigger. That means stepping offline, parrying or striking the weapon-bearing limb, and collapsing into the attacker with full-body pressure. From there, strikes, controls, or takedowns may follow—but the first goal is always to neutralize the weapon's trajectory. You cannot fight back if you're dead.

Edged weapons are even more insidious. A knife is easy to conceal, easy to deploy, and devastating at close range. Unlike guns, they don't jam, don't run out of ammo, and don't make noise. In a sudden attack, you may not even see the blade until it's cutting you. That's why blade defense must be trained as if the attacker *is already cutting*—because that's usually how it starts.

Disarming a knife-wielding attacker is not about catching the blade. It's about controlling the limb, disrupting their structure, and inflicting enough damage to create disengagement or unconsciousness. You must crash in—parrying the limb, striking the attacker's face, neck, or legs, and taking control of their base. A knife fight is not a duel. It is a sprint. You will likely be cut. Your goal is to be cut *less*, and to end the fight *sooner*.

Because disarming is so dangerous, sometimes the better option is to arm *yourself*—not with a weapon you brought, but with one you find. This is where improvised weapon deployment comes in.

Every environment has tools. Chairs, bottles, pens, keys, umbrellas, belts, cookware, flashlights, even books. The key is not what the object is, but how quickly you recognize it as a force multiplier and how effectively you can deploy it under stress.

Improvised weapon deployment requires three things: awareness, access, and intent. You must train yourself to see objects *before* you need them, to know where your hands will go in a panic, and to use that object as if it was designed for violence—even if it wasn't. A heavy flashlight to the skull can knock a man unconscious. A coffee mug to the face can break teeth. A rolled-up magazine can target the throat. In that moment, you are not improvising. You are *weaponizing* the world around you.

Disarmament and retention are not passive concepts. They are active responses to active danger. They are not glamorous. They are not safe. But they are necessary. Because when weapons enter the fight, everything accelerates—pain, injury, consequences. There's no room for theory. Only execution.

In real violence, the only rule is this: the person who controls the weapon controls the outcome.

Chapter 5: Tactical Use of Force Continuum

"Violence of action, speed, and surprise are the key elements of successful assault."
— U.S. Army Field Manual

5.1 De-escalation When Possible

The most effective fighters are not those who seek conflict, but those who understand the full spectrum of violence—when to apply it, how much to apply, and most importantly, when to avoid it entirely. In a world filled with unpredictable variables, legal consequences, and the potential for irreversible outcomes, restraint is often the highest expression of tactical skill. De-escalation, therefore, is not weakness. It is the discipline of a professional, the foresight of someone who knows that survival is not only about physical victory, but about emerging from a threat intact—physically, legally, and morally.

Before fists are thrown or weapons drawn, most confrontations offer a window of negotiation. This window may be seconds wide, or it may be stretched across several minutes of building tension. Inside that window lies the opportunity to prevent violence through words, posture, tone, and psychological maneuvering. The foundation of this art lies in a concept often referred to as "verbal judo," a system of persuasive communication that redirects aggression, diffuses hostility, and offers the aggressor a path out—without feeling like they lost.

Verbal judo begins with control of the self. If your voice trembles, your face flushes with anger, or your tone becomes reactive, you've already ceded ground. The first target in any de-escalation scenario is your own physiology. You must breathe slowly, speak deliberately, and maintain a tone that is firm without being aggressive. The moment you allow yourself to escalate emotionally, you fuel the confrontation. The objective is not to out-argue or dominate the other person. It's to regain control of the emotional tempo and guide it toward resolution.

In confrontational situations, people don't usually respond to logic. They respond to how they're made to feel. If they feel disrespected, humiliated, or cornered, their aggression increases—even if your words are reasonable. That's why tone, pacing, and body language matter as much as, if not more than, the content of your speech. Verbal judo practitioners often mirror the cadence of the aggressor initially, then slowly lower their tone and tempo, drawing the other person into a calmer rhythm without them realizing it. This subtle shift recalibrates the encounter, and in many cases, the aggressor unconsciously de-escalates to match your energy.

The language you use must be both clear and tactically selected. Direct threats invite resistance. Sarcasm invites escalation. Orders often provoke defiance. Instead, you offer choices that preserve the aggressor's dignity while guiding the encounter away from danger. Instead of "Back off or I'll call the cops," you say, "Let's not turn this into something we both regret." You replace commands with options, ultimatums with suggestions. The goal is to plant a seed: that backing down isn't a loss of face, it's a wise decision. That continuing will bring costs, but walking away still leaves them in control.

These linguistic redirections must be supported by body language that aligns with the message. If your words are calming but your posture is aggressive—clenched fists, squared shoulders, forward-leaning stance—you send mixed signals. The subconscious mind reads body language faster than it processes speech, and any inconsistency undermines your credibility. Effective de-escalators adopt a neutral stance: feet shoulder-width apart, hands visible and open, chest angled slightly away to reduce perceived threat, head upright but not tilted downward. This posture conveys readiness without provocation.

Where you position yourself in relation to the aggressor also matters. Standing directly in front of someone, especially close, is often interpreted as a challenge. Angling your body, stepping to the side slightly, or maintaining a respectful distance communicates that you're not looking for a fight. It gives the other person space—literal and psychological—to make a different choice. At the same time, you must remain aware of your surroundings. De-escalation is not pacifism. You are still preparing for the possibility of violence, tracking exits, gauging their movements, and noting changes in tone or proximity.

In certain situations, de-escalation must go further than soothing language and non-threatening posture. It must offer the aggressor a *face-saving exit*. People escalate not just because they're angry, but because they feel trapped—socially, emotionally, or reputationally. If you can give them a way out that preserves their image or authority, they are more likely to take it. This is especially important in public settings, group dynamics, or when the aggressor is under the influence of ego, alcohol, or peer pressure.

Offering such exits requires finesse. You might say, "I get it, you've had a long night, we've all been there. Let's just call it even." Or, "You're clearly having a rough day, and I don't want to add to it. Let's both walk away before this gets worse." These statements allow the aggressor to de-escalate without surrendering pride. It reframes the conflict not as a loss, but as a decision made from strength or maturity.

In some cases, the exit strategy may involve physically disengaging. If the conversation is going nowhere and the tension is rising, it's better to leave—if you can do so safely—than to wait for the storm to break. This requires situational awareness: knowing your exits, being able to move without turning your back, avoiding sudden motions that might trigger a reaction. You may need to speak as you go, to soften the movement: "We're clearly not going to agree, I'll leave you to it," or, "You've made your point, I'm out of here." These lines allow for disengagement without challenging the other person's authority or escalating the situation.

But not all de-escalation efforts succeed. Some people want a fight. Some are too intoxicated, enraged, or unstable to reason with. That's why de-escalation should never be your *only* strategy—it should be your *first* one. Your posture, words, and demeanor should say: "I don't want to fight, but I will if I have to." That balance—between calm and readiness, between peace and strength—is what makes de-escalation effective. If you project only passivity, the aggressor may interpret it as weakness. If you project only threat, you may provoke them further. The balance is delicate, but trainable.

Professionals in law enforcement, executive protection, and crisis negotiation spend countless hours rehearsing these interactions—not because they are afraid to fight, but because they understand that *not* fighting, when possible, is the best outcome. Every act of de-escalation that prevents injury, arrest, or trauma is a success. It means your training worked. It means you had the presence of mind to manage not just the threat, but the moment.

De-escalation also extends beyond the stranger in a parking lot or the belligerent man at the bar. It applies to domestic disputes, workplace confrontations, road rage, and even verbal disagreements that start to boil over. The same principles apply: lower the temperature, preserve dignity, manage posture, provide exits. When you practice de-escalation regularly—when it becomes part of how you carry yourself—you'll find that people react to you differently. They'll sense the quiet confidence, the presence, the control. And that alone is often enough to prevent escalation from starting in the first place.

Some may believe that preparing for violence means focusing only on strikes, weapons, and tactics. But that is only half of the path. The other half—the one that prevents unnecessary destruction—is built on communication, emotional control, and psychological strategy. True warriors know when to act. Greater warriors know when *not* to.

5.2 Escalation of Force Protocols

There are moments when words fail. When tone, posture, and diplomacy dissolve into irrelevance because the threat in front of you is not interested in talking. These are the moments when self-defense becomes action. But action without direction is chaos. In the realm of civilian defense, you don't just need to know how to protect yourself—you need to know *how much* protection is legally and ethically justified. Because what you do in the next three seconds might save your life… or destroy it.

Understanding when you are legally permitted to use force, and how much force is justified, isn't an academic concern. It's a survival skill. After the confrontation ends, someone will ask what happened. If the attacker is injured or dead, the burden of explanation will likely fall on you. The difference between justified self-defense and criminal assault often comes down to how you explain what you did, and whether your actions aligned with recognized standards of proportionality and necessity.

R.A.T. Fight

In most jurisdictions, the law grants individuals the right to use force when they reasonably believe it is necessary to protect themselves or others from imminent harm. This isn't based on whether harm actually occurred—it's about what a reasonable person, in your exact situation, would have believed. That phrase—*reasonable belief*—is the cornerstone of lawful self-defense. It means your perception of the threat matters, but it must be grounded in what the average person would consider credible, not just your personal fear or anger.

But legality doesn't end with *whether* force was used—it also hinges on *how much* force was used. A punch thrown in response to a shove may be seen as reasonable. A fatal blow delivered after the threat has turned to run may be seen as criminal. Proportional response is the bridge between necessity and excess. You are permitted to defend yourself, but only to the degree that your defense matches the threat.

This is where training becomes more than physical. You must develop the ability to *read* a situation in real time and apply force accordingly. If someone yells in your face but makes no physical move, you have the right to disengage—not to strike. If someone grabs your wrist, a violent break may be excessive. But if that grab is followed by a punch, your justification increases. If a weapon is drawn or you're cornered by multiple aggressors, the law gives you wider latitude. But even then, the question remains: did you stop when the threat stopped?

Self-defense is not revenge. It is not punishment. It is interruption. It is force applied only long enough to end the danger. That distinction becomes critical in the courtroom and in your own conscience. Once the attacker is no longer a threat—whether because they've fled, fallen, or surrendered—your right to use force ends. Continuing to strike at that point becomes retaliation, not protection, and it crosses the line into criminal conduct.

This is why *warning systems* matter—not just tactically, but legally. Verbal warnings, physical signals, and behavioral cues can serve a dual purpose. They may actually deter the aggressor, but they also create a record of your intent. If witnesses hear you say "Back off" or "I don't want to fight," that statement becomes evidence that you attempted to de-escalate. If surveillance footage shows you with hands raised in a non-threatening posture, it supports your claim that you were not the aggressor. These cues won't guarantee protection from legal scrutiny, but they help build a narrative that aligns with lawful self-defense.

Even in the heat of confrontation, these signals can be delivered without weakness. Saying "Leave now" in a firm, confident voice is not pleading—it's warning. Holding your hands up, palms visible, while stepping back does not mean you're surrendering—it shows you're seeking to avoid harm while maintaining readiness. If force then becomes necessary, you've demonstrated that it was a last resort, not your first instinct.

Escalation of force is not a linear process. It can skip stages. You might go from verbal exchange to life-threatening violence in seconds. But whenever possible, you want your progression to reflect restraint. Start with disengagement. Move to assertive communication. Shift to non-lethal defense. Escalate only as far as the threat demands—and no further. If your attacker has a weapon, you're justified in responding with lethal force. If they're unarmed but charging, you're justified in using whatever force stops them without going beyond necessity.

Context matters. Location, witnesses, your physical condition, the presence of others—all shape how your actions will be interpreted. A disabled individual defending against an able-bodied attacker may be given more latitude. A parent protecting their child may be judged differently than someone defending property. These nuances must be understood, not assumed.

Training must include these ethical and legal scenarios. You must not only practice punches and takedowns—you must rehearse *judgment*. Because real violence comes fast, but the consequences unfold slowly. In the seconds it takes to throw a strike, you may shape years of your future. That is why escalation protocols are not theoretical—they are embedded in every decision you make in a confrontation. Your goal is to win the moment and survive the aftermath.

5.3 Maximum Violence When Required

There are some moments that exist outside the spectrum of negotiation, reason, or calibration. Moments when survival hangs by a thread, when hesitation equals death, and when your only path forward is overwhelming violence delivered with speed, surprise, and absolute commitment. In these moments, the measured steps of force escalation give way to the final stage: total domination of the threat through whatever means necessary. This is where the concept of the *violence switch* becomes real.

Most people live their entire lives without flipping that switch. Some don't even know they have it. But it exists in all of us—the latent capacity to shed restraint and unleash force when cornered. This isn't about rage. It isn't about emotional explosion. It's about a calculated, trained ability to move with devastating aggression when survival demands it.

The violence switch is not something that flips easily, nor should it. In civilized society, we are trained to suppress aggression, to de-escalate, to submit to authority and avoid confrontation. But in an ambush, in a kidnapping attempt, in a home invasion, there is no time for civility. The attacker has already chosen the rules of engagement. Your only job is to *survive*. And that means shifting from defense to offense with immediate intensity.

This shift must be rehearsed—not fantasized, but built through realistic training. You must become familiar with the rhythm of explosive action. It means driving through the threat, not backing away. It means moving faster and harder than your opponent can process. The goal is not just to stop the attack—it is to overwhelm it so completely that the attacker has no chance to regroup.

When facing multiple attackers, this principle becomes even more critical. You cannot afford to engage all threats equally. You must prioritize. You must identify the most dangerous attacker—the one closest, the one with the weapon, the one showing the most aggression—and eliminate or disable them first. This is *target prioritization*, and it's how trained professionals handle chaos. The goal is to break the cohesion of the group, to make them scatter, to turn their numbers into confusion.

Engaging multiple threats doesn't mean standing in the center and fighting like a movie hero. It means moving. Constantly. You find angles. You use obstacles. You deny flanks. You strike with brutal intent and then reposition before the others can react. You never allow yourself to be surrounded. You use the environment—walls, cars, furniture—not just for cover but for control. Every step is calculated to preserve mobility and disrupt coordination.

Against multiple threats, hesitation is fatal. If you wait to see who moves first, they win. Your violence must be immediate, shocking, and strategic. One attacker goes down. The others hesitate. That hesitation buys you time. Time to escape. Time to continue fighting on your terms. Time to survive.

But violence must have an *end point*. Once the threat is neutralized, you must stop. This is what professionals call *termination criteria*. It's the moment when force is no longer necessary, and continued action becomes excessive. If the attacker is unconscious, disabled, or fleeing, and you continue to strike, you shift from defender to assailant. Not just morally, but legally.

Knowing when to stop is as important as knowing when to start. That awareness is the difference between justice and vengeance. Between a justified action and a charge of excessive force. It also protects you psychologically. Because carrying the weight of necessary violence is difficult enough. Carrying the weight of unnecessary violence is something else entirely.

In training, this means building the habit of constant assessment. Even in high-stress drills, you should be asking yourself: is the threat still active? Are they still armed? Are they retreating? Can I disengage safely? That habit becomes instinct, and instinct becomes your guide when your brain is overwhelmed.

Maximum violence is not about inflicting harm—it's about eliminating the threat with finality. It is controlled, deliberate, and unrelenting. It is the culmination of every layer of the force continuum. And it must be followed by restraint. That balance—between fury and control, between chaos and discipline—is what makes a warrior, not a brute.

There will be situations where only violence saves you. In those moments, you cannot pause. You cannot second-guess. You must become the storm. But when the storm passes, you must also have the clarity to step back into yourself—to disengage, to breathe, to recover, and to live with what was necessary.

That is the burden and the responsibility of those who train for the worst. To be capable of destruction, but never to crave it. To be violent only when survival demands it—and to stop the moment it no longer does.

Chapter 6: Weapons of Opportunity

"Anything can be a weapon if you hold it right."
— Clive Barker

6.1 Environmental Weapon Assessment

When most people hear the word "weapon," they think of the obvious: guns, knives, batons, pepper spray. But real-world violence rarely offers the convenience of preparedness. You will not always be armed when danger arrives. You may be in a place where carrying a weapon is illegal or socially unacceptable. You may be ambushed, blindsided, or caught in a location where retrieving your gear is impossible. In such moments, your ability to identify, access, and use your environment as a source of tools can mean the difference between helplessness and survival. The concept of "weapons of opportunity" is not philosophical. It is tactical. And it begins with learning to see the world not as passive scenery—but as an arsenal.

Environmental weapon assessment is the art of scanning any space and asking the question: What here could hurt someone if used with intent? The answer is almost always "plenty." Most people simply don't notice. Their eyes are trained to see function and familiarity. A coffee cup is for drinking. A pen is for writing. A chair is for sitting. But in the hands of someone trained to think tactically, every object takes on new dimension. A coffee cup becomes a blunt instrument. A pen becomes a stabbing tool. A chair becomes a barrier, a ram, or even a makeshift shield. The object's original purpose is irrelevant. What matters is what *you* can do with it.

R.A.T. Fight

Let's begin with the urban environment—offices, restaurants, transportation hubs, public buildings, and parking structures. These are the most common locations where people spend their daily lives and, paradoxically, where they are often least prepared to defend themselves. Yet they are filled with potential weapons if you know what to look for.

In an office, the average desk contains multiple items that can be repurposed for defense. Pens and pencils can be used to target soft tissue areas like the eyes, throat, or hands. Scissors, if available, need no explanation. A heavy stapler or tape dispenser becomes an instant striking tool. Even a ceramic coffee mug, swung by the handle or shattered and gripped with fabric, becomes an edge weapon capable of inflicting serious injury.

Chairs, particularly rolling office chairs or rigid visitor chairs, can be used to create distance, break line of sight, or push an assailant into walls or corners. The metal arms or legs of such furniture can be driven into the attacker's shins or knees. A full overhead strike using a chair as a bludgeon can stop forward momentum. Monitor cords or laptop charging cables can be used as flexible weapons for entanglement or choking, though extreme caution is needed in their deployment.

In restaurants or cafés, you are surrounded by glass, cutlery, and dense objects. A drinking glass shattered on a table edge becomes a jagged tool. A butter knife may not look intimidating, but when driven into sensitive tissue at close range, it can be effective. A dinner plate, held like a frisbee, can be thrown to distract or break contact. Cloth napkins wrapped around the hand allow you to grip hot or sharp items, or even punch without losing knuckle integrity. Metal forks or skewers can be gripped tightly and used for gouging or stabbing motions.

Bars present another wealth of options. Bottles, especially full ones, offer significant kinetic energy when swung. Even plastic cocktail stirrers, broken and used with surprise, can jab into soft targets. Barstools offer mobility and elevation. A belt pulled rapidly from your waist can become a whip, a garrote, or an entanglement device. Doormen often use pool cues not for playing, but for spacing control—something to consider if you're ever in a pool hall and need a quick reach advantage.

Parking lots are typically seen as open, empty, and vulnerable places. But they offer opportunities too. A car key can be gripped between fingers or held in an icepick grip for striking. A seatbelt buckle, if you're inside your car, becomes a flail. The steel rod of a tire iron or a windshield scraper offers tremendous leverage. Shopping carts can be used to block, push, or create a barrier. Even a plastic water bottle, when frozen or filled, delivers significant blunt force.

Public transportation presents the challenge of confined space but provides other unique tools. Vertical poles on buses and trains can be used to trap, pivot, or slam an attacker. Backpacks, even light ones, can be swung like maces or used as a shield. Earbuds with cords can be turned into impromptu binding tools, particularly in chokeholds. Laptops, hardbound books, and even steel water bottles have enough density to stun if used with speed and surprise.

And yet, the world doesn't just offer man-made objects. It offers structural features that, with the right mindset, can be just as deadly. Stairs become throwing platforms. A fall down a staircase can end a fight immediately, especially if the attacker is off-balance. Doorframes can be used to trap arms. Walls can be used for head strikes, shoulder slams, or joint breaks. Even curbs or concrete parking blocks can be used to destabilize the knees, shins, or ankles of an attacker. A foot stomp delivered with force while someone is walking backward onto a curb can result in a broken ankle or complete collapse.

Furniture—especially in homes, lounges, or waiting rooms—offers leverage. Couch cushions can be shoved into faces for disorientation or used to obscure vision. Table edges can be used for limb breaks or slams. Bookcases can be tipped. Drawers can be slammed. Bathroom stalls offer door hinges, mop buckets, porcelain sinks. Every surface, every shape, becomes a tool in the hands of someone who refuses to be passive.

But not every situation allows for aggression with environmental weapons. Sometimes, legality or social context demands that you carry *something*, without it being recognized as a weapon. That's where concealed carry alternatives become essential.

In jurisdictions where traditional weapons are restricted, people turn to disguised or dual-use items. Tactical pens made of aluminum are indistinguishable from ordinary pens but can be used to strike or stab. Flashlights—especially small, dense ones—double as palm impact tools and often go unnoticed during security checks. Canes, umbrellas, or even dog leashes can be used as striking tools, hooks, or whips. Paracord bracelets or keychains with hardened beads serve as flails or pressure tools.

Legal self-defense tools like pepper gel or spray are also essential considerations. In some areas, traditional pepper spray may be restricted, but gel-based versions or small animal-defense sprays may be permitted. The key is to understand local laws and work within them while maximizing your personal security.

Environmental weapons also rely on your mental presence. You must train yourself to scan every room you enter. When you sit down, ask: what can I reach? What can I throw? What can I shield myself with? Where are the exit paths, and what in this environment can I use to shape them in my favor? The habit doesn't require paranoia—only awareness. It turns the world into an extension of your arsenal.

One critical concept to remember is *adaptation under stress*. It's one thing to spot a wine bottle in a restaurant. It's another to grab it, grip it correctly, and swing it effectively when your hands are shaking, your heart is racing, and your body is screaming for survival. This is why training with improvised weapons must become part of your self-defense regimen. Not every session, but regularly. Practice picking up random items and experimenting with strikes, grips, angles. Learn how to break a bottle safely. Learn how to grip a pen without dropping it during a stabbing motion. Learn how to throw a chair to distract, not just to hit.

The true essence of environmental weapon assessment lies not in what you hold—but in *how* you hold it. It's the intent that weaponizes the object. The tactical mind sees beyond labels and appearances. It recognizes that in the chaos of violence, control belongs to the one who adapts first. A piece of trash becomes a blinding distraction. A rolled magazine becomes a windpipe disruptor. A coffee mug becomes a jawbreaker.

Your body is the primary weapon. But your environment is your ally. And when the two move together with intent and awareness, your chances of survival increase exponentially.

6.2 Improvised Weapon Construction

Improvisation in violence is not an act of desperation—it's an art form honed through necessity, forged by experience, and validated by survival. The ability to turn ordinary objects into tools of defense under extreme pressure is not reserved for the battlefield or espionage fiction. It is a real-world skill used by everyone from special operations personnel in denied-access environments to civilians caught unarmed in the wrong place at the wrong time. When violence is imminent and traditional weapons are unavailable or illegal, the environment becomes your workshop, and speed becomes your greatest asset.

Field expedient weapons are devices created quickly from items in your immediate surroundings—items that would not typically be considered threatening. What makes them dangerous is your intent, your knowledge of body mechanics, and your ability to construct and deploy them before the situation unfolds past your control. In the realm of military and special forces doctrine, field expedient weaponry is taught not as a last resort, but as a default mindset. If a combative situation is anticipated in a space where known tools aren't permitted, you are expected to craft something effective before engagement begins.

This can be as simple as wrapping a rock in a sock and tying it off into a flail that delivers crushing blows with minimal risk to the hand. In an urban setting, a similar effect can be achieved using a padlock and a length of cable, or even a water bottle filled with coins or sand. The tool doesn't need to last. It needs to work—once or twice, long enough to create escape or establish dominance.

Improvised spears can be crafted using broom handles or umbrella shafts with attached glass shards, cutlery, or even sharpened plastic. A pencil reinforced with tape around the base can provide additional grip and reduce breakage during impact. In prison systems around the world, inmates fashion tools from toothbrushes, razors, paper, and melted plastic—proof that when people are deprived of conventional tools, innovation becomes instinct.

The key to building effective improvised weapons is understanding the balance between concealability, accessibility, and lethality. A weapon that takes too long to assemble, or that can't be carried discreetly, loses value in most civilian settings. That's where modification techniques come into play. These are subtle adjustments to everyday objects that enhance their defensive potential without making them obvious weapons.

For instance, a flashlight with a beveled edge can serve both as a utility tool and an impact weapon. Adding weight to the handle or wrapping it with paracord increases grip and kinetic output. A standard ballpoint pen can be replaced with a tactical pen made of aircraft-grade aluminum, which functions identically as a writing tool but offers a solid striking point capable of breaking glass or disabling an attacker with a thrust to the eye, neck, or temple.

Even innocuous items like a cane or walking stick can be retrofitted with hardened tips, rubber grips, or internal weights. An umbrella with a reinforced shaft becomes a stabbing tool when held in reverse. Shoelaces or cords with attached washers, nuts, or heavy beads become quick, concealable flails that are indistinguishable from fashion accessories until deployed.

One of the more advanced concepts in modification is dual-purpose construction. This involves selecting or altering personal items in a way that allows them to serve their regular function while also being instantly usable in a combative context. A steel water bottle can be chosen for its weight and durability, allowing for blunt force strikes while still serving as a hydration tool. A belt with a large, dense buckle can function as a distraction tool, whip, or entanglement device, while remaining indistinguishable from standard attire.

The genius of modification lies in its subtlety. You are not advertising danger. You are not carrying anything that would raise suspicion in a pat-down or airport security setting. But in the moment of need, your "harmless" item becomes a tool of survival—because you built it that way.

R.A.T. Fight

The final piece of improvised weapon construction is deployment strategy. Having a tool is meaningless if you can't get to it, wield it properly, and apply it under stress. This is where most people fail—not in the construction of tools, but in the use of them when adrenaline floods the body and motor control degrades.

Deployment begins with access. Wherever your improvised weapon is stored—bag, pocket, waistband, shoe—it must be reachable with either hand, ideally without looking. If your setup requires precision or both hands working in tandem, it will likely fail when stress peaks. You must train your draw as if you were drawing a firearm. The hand should move naturally to the object, extract it cleanly, and immediately prepare to use it—without delay or confusion.

Once drawn, the weapon must be usable from multiple grips and angles. A hammer-style grip might work for stabbing or swinging downward, while an icepick grip may allow more control in tight spaces. You must be able to transition between offensive strikes and defensive postures fluidly, using the weapon to shield, block, and distract as needed.

Maintaining the element of surprise is a tactical advantage, especially when the attacker assumes you are unarmed. If you can deploy an improvised weapon from concealment while speaking or moving, you may gain the half-second needed to strike first and shift the dynamic. A sudden burst of movement combined with the reveal of a tool—something as simple as a pen clutched in the hand—can break the attacker's rhythm and force a recalculation. That window is where your survival lives.

The construction, modification, and deployment of improvised weapons must not be left to chance. Like any skill, it demands repetition, experimentation, and evaluation. You must walk through the environments you occupy daily—home, office, car, gym—and ask yourself: What's here? What can be made? How fast can I get to it? What will I do with it?

Preparedness is not paranoia. It is readiness disguised as normalcy. The world is full of tools. It is your responsibility to make them yours.

6.3 Weapon Effectiveness and Limitations

All weapons—conventional or improvised—come with their own limitations. There is no perfect tool, no universal solution to all threats. Effectiveness is always contextual. What works in a hallway may fail in a car. What succeeds against one attacker may prove disastrous against many. To wield a weapon intelligently, you must not only understand how to use it, but also where it thrives, where it fails, and what you risk by relying on it.

Impact weapons—those designed to cause trauma through blunt force—are among the most accessible and intuitive forms of defense. From clubs and pipes to flashlights and crowbars, their goal is to transmit kinetic energy into the body of an attacker, creating disruption, disorientation, or unconsciousness. The science is simple: mass multiplied by speed equals force. When directed into vulnerable areas—head, jaw, knees, ribs—that force causes the attacker's structure or awareness to collapse.

But impact weapons are only effective if you know how to deliver them correctly. Striking the skull at the wrong angle may cause injury, but not enough to stop the threat. Hitting a heavily muscled area may only irritate. You must understand targeting. The jawline, when struck laterally, often leads to unconsciousness due to the rotational trauma to the brain. The side of the neck can compromise blood flow or breathing. Knees, when struck from the outside, collapse posture. Shins and fingers, though smaller targets, carry high nerve density and can disrupt grip and balance.

Still, impact weapons carry a legal and moral risk. The line between justified force and excessive damage is thin. Blunt trauma can lead to permanent injury or death, especially when delivered to the head. Courts and juries will ask whether your use of force was proportionate. You must be able to justify your actions not only through what happened, but through how you interpreted the threat.

Cutting and stabbing implements, whether improvised or conventional, carry even greater risks and responsibilities. A blade or sharp object introduces the potential for lethal damage quickly. Slashes to the arms or legs can sever tendons or arteries. Stabs to the torso or neck can be fatal. Because of this, edged weapons are often classified legally as lethal force tools, and their use may be scrutinized even more heavily than blunt force options.

Technique with edged weapons is about control, not frenzy. Wild slashing rarely achieves clean results and often leads to the defender injuring themselves. A forward stabbing motion, delivered with the whole body behind it, creates deep penetration. Angled thrusts or raking motions target soft tissue. Gripping the weapon tightly and protecting the wrist is crucial, especially if the tool is not designed for combat. A pen may snap. A broken bottle may cut the wielder's hand. Your goal is to inflict damage without disabling yourself.

The decision to use a cutting implement should be reserved for moments where no other option exists. The presence of a blade escalates the confrontation instantly. It signals lethal intent, whether or not that was your purpose. This must be weighed carefully—not just in the moment, but in the courtroom that may follow.

Not all weapons need to wound. Some need only to *disable*—to create distraction, to impair, to open a window for escape. This is the realm of legal chemical and irritant tools: pepper sprays, tear gas, gels, foams, and dye markers. These substances, when deployed correctly, do not rely on physical contact. They work by targeting the senses—blinding, choking, confusing the attacker enough to break the rhythm of assault.

Pepper spray, for instance, causes immediate inflammation of the eyes, throat, and skin. The attacker may cough, stumble, or retreat. But effectiveness depends on deployment. Spraying against the wind, or from too far a distance, renders it useless. Accuracy and timing are essential. Gels and foams reduce blowback but require closer range. Some sprays include UV dye to mark attackers for later identification.

Chemical options carry fewer legal complications in most regions, though their use must still be justified. Spraying someone because they shouted or pushed you will likely be viewed as disproportionate. But deploying it during an attempted mugging or assault—especially with warning—can fall well within legal bounds.

The final category of nonlethal weapons includes distraction tools. Flashbang-type devices, loud alarms, or personal defense sirens are not weapons in the traditional sense, but they create confusion and buy time. A piercing noise in a parking garage may send an attacker running. A sudden burst of light may give you the half-second needed to flee.

The key is knowing the purpose of your tool. Some are designed to *finish* the fight. Others are designed to *end* your participation in it. Some give you dominance. Others give you distance.

Effectiveness is about choosing the right tool for the right moment—and accepting the consequences that come with its use.

Every weapon is a decision. Not just a tactical one, but an ethical one. Your survival matters. But so does your ability to live with what you did to survive.

Chapter 7: Team Tactics and Group Dynamics

"No plan survives contact with the enemy, but planning survives contact with the enemy."
— Dwight D. Eisenhower

7.1 Multiple Attacker Scenarios

Violence is rarely fair. It does not conform to the choreographed ideals seen in martial arts competitions or cinematic brawls where opponents wait their turn. In the real world, when an attack unfolds in public spaces, homes, alleys, or chaotic protests, it's not unusual for violence to come from more than one direction. Multiple attacker scenarios are not just statistically common in criminal assaults—they are logistically inevitable when aggression happens in areas where people move in groups. Street fights, gang initiations, home invasions, flash mobs, riots, or simply being in the wrong place when tensions flare can thrust an individual into a situation where fighting back doesn't mean facing one threat—it means managing several.

The challenge of dealing with multiple attackers is not merely quantitative—it's qualitative. The physics of the fight change. Your movement must now account for spatial control, environmental hazards, shifting momentum, and the psychology of group dynamics. Most importantly, the margin for error narrows to almost nothing. A split-second delay, a misjudged angle, a commitment to the wrong target, and you are flanked or pinned before you can course-correct. In these moments, the only path forward lies in your ability to think with clarity, move with purpose, and prioritize with ruthless efficiency.

R.A.T. Fight

Before anything else, you must establish a clear threat hierarchy. This is not a moral decision. It's a survival one. In any group of aggressors, someone is the leader—or at least the most immediately dangerous. This might be the individual who initiates contact, the one who holds a weapon, or the person whose body language shows confidence and control while the others wait or watch. Your first job is to identify this individual and make them your priority. Neutralizing the strongest threat early—whether through evasion, incapacitation, or psychological disruption—creates a vacuum in the group dynamic. When the others see their alpha falter, fear, confusion, or hesitation often sets in.

This is not speculation—it's behaviorally documented. Group violence often hinges on imitation and momentum. When the leader advances, the others follow. When that momentum breaks, the followers scatter or become far less committed. A precise, explosive engagement that stuns or drops the most confident attacker is often enough to unhinge the rest. This doesn't mean you aim for theatrics. It means you aim for results. Disable decisively. Move immediately.

Your movement in multi-attacker scenarios must be governed by a simple principle: never allow yourself to be surrounded. A single opponent in front of you can be dealt with. An attacker behind you while another closes from the front creates a pincer you may not escape. The human body, even with excellent peripheral awareness, cannot fully monitor 360 degrees. That means your positioning must constantly reorient your blind spots toward neutral zones—walls, locked doors, parked cars, or any obstacle that prevents access from one side.

In open spaces, your movement should create angles rather than lines. Instead of backing up in a straight path—which may trap you or cause you to trip—you pivot diagonally, moving around attackers rather than away from them. Each motion should be dual-purpose: escape one reach while positioning for a counter on another. Your footwork becomes as important as your strikes. Every step buys you a second more to think and react.

Using the environment is not optional—it's essential. A parked car, a stairwell, a column, or even a large trash bin can break sightlines and funnel attackers into a narrower space, where their numbers work against them. In tactical training, this is known as "funneling"—forcing adversaries into single-file engagement by positioning yourself where only one or two can reach you at a time. This is how professional bodyguards escort clients through hostile crowds: not by fighting their way out, but by manipulating terrain to limit exposure.

Even in less favorable environments—like an open hallway or courtyard—your movement should create micro-barriers. Step behind a chair. Knock over a table. Position a large person between yourself and the others, using their hesitation to strike a cleaner angle or find a break in their formation.

But movement alone won't save you. You need to divide the problem. "Divide and conquer" is not just a battlefield slogan—it's a neurological and physical imperative. When multiple attackers converge, their strength lies in cooperation. If you can break that cohesion—through fear, confusion, or sheer aggression—you create openings. This doesn't always mean you physically separate them. Sometimes you manipulate psychology instead.

Targeting the first attacker with overwhelming violence—whether that's a flurry of strikes, a thrown object, or even a moment of erratic movement—can startle the others. Most people aren't truly committed to violence. They go along with it. When they see one of their own go down hard, the emotional contract begins to unravel. Some will freeze. Others will posture instead of act. A few may flee outright.

Another way to divide is to use speed. If attackers are approaching from multiple angles but haven't yet surrounded you, you may have a brief window where you can rush one before the others catch up. That moment—however short—can be exploited to eliminate one threat quickly. It might be a strike to the knee that drops someone long enough for you to move past. It might be a push into a wall. The goal is to prevent all attackers from engaging simultaneously.

However, this tactic comes with risks. Closing distance on one target may expose you to another. That's why your follow-through matters. You don't just hit and stand still. You hit and move. A strike that ends in a side-step or spin shifts your body's axis away from the others. A shove that redirects one attacker into another forces a micro-collision. Movement is not a break between strikes—it is the strike's continuation.

The presence of weapons changes the landscape dramatically. If one of the attackers has a blade, a blunt object, or worse, a firearm, your priorities must adjust instantly. The armed individual becomes your focus unless the weapon is visibly passive. A man holding a bottle but making no move toward you might be less of a concern than a man reaching behind his waistband. You must gauge intent by watching the hands, the eyes, and the torso—where tension gathers before action. If you miss the cue, you'll be too late.

Fighting multiple attackers while unarmed requires a brutal economy of energy. You cannot afford fancy techniques or extended engagements. Every motion must serve survival. This means favoring gross motor actions—palm strikes, elbow drives, low kicks, eye gouges—over techniques that rely on fine motor precision. The fight must be short, explosive, and directional. You are not there to win. You are there to get out.

Verbal tactics can also play a subtle role. Screaming commands like "BACK OFF!" or "CALL 911!" not only draw attention from others nearby, but may psychologically shift the attackers into doubt. It introduces unpredictability. It signals that you're not passive prey. In some cases, aggressors will hesitate if they think others are watching, or if they believe you are not alone.

There's also a level of internal clarity required for this kind of chaos. Panic is the enemy of decisiveness. You must train, not just physically, but mentally, to accept that these scenarios are survivable. The mind must be drilled to seek patterns amid noise, to ignore the unimportant, and to make rapid choices under pressure. Training for multi-attacker scenarios must involve unpredictability, fluidity, and the integration of environmental interaction. It must simulate not just movement and strikes, but confusion, fatigue, and rapid recalibration.

In the end, fighting multiple attackers is not about heroism or dominance. It is about disrupting the timeline of violence long enough to find or create your exit. The objective is not to "win" in the sense of defeating everyone present. The objective is to stay mobile, stay thinking, and stay alive.

If you are in a position where confrontation is inevitable, and the numbers are not in your favor, your brain becomes your most lethal weapon. Every decision you make either narrows your options or expands them. Every step, every look, every strike must be made not with panic, but with precision born from preparation. You won't get a second chance to be ready. The plan may not survive the fight—but your training will.

7.2 Protecting Others

There is a marked difference between surviving violence alone and surviving violence with others depending on you. When you are responsible not just for your own life but for the lives of loved ones, friends, or even strangers, your priorities and tactics must shift. The presence of non-combatants—especially those unable to defend themselves—introduces a layer of complexity that can break even seasoned professionals if unprepared. The ability to protect others is not innate; it is trained, rehearsed, and deliberately built into your decision-making process.

At the core of protective action lies a mindset of self-sacrifice married with strategic clarity. You are no longer just avoiding danger or neutralizing threats. You are directing movement, shielding bodies, and often absorbing the chaos that would otherwise engulf the untrained. This requires not only technical ability but the presence of mind to act as a human buffer—both physical and psychological—between danger and those in your care.

One of the most critical concepts borrowed from military and executive protection training is the use of movement formations. In hostile environments, bodyguards rarely walk randomly through crowds. Their placement is specific, coordinated, and based on a constant threat assessment that adapts in real-time. These principles apply just as powerfully in a civilian setting. Whether you are escorting children through a protest that's turned volatile or guiding your spouse out of a mall during a violent incident, how you position yourself and those you're protecting can determine the outcome.

A simple but effective model involves placing yourself between the threat and the people you're protecting. If the threat is unknown, this means taking a rear or perimeter position while placing them slightly ahead and within your field of control. If the threat is specific and directional—say, a violent individual approaching from the front—you shift into the frontmost role, absorbing attention and preparing to intercept. This can involve extending an arm to keep someone behind you or using environmental obstacles as partial cover.

When under threat, movement becomes the most vital tool. You are not looking to engage unless necessary; you are looking to extract. The longer you stay in the hot zone, the more opportunities danger has to evolve. Therefore, evacuation procedures must be drilled into your personal operating system. You need to know where the exits are, not just physically but functionally—where they lead, whether they're likely to be jammed, whether they lock from one side or both.

Evacuation is not just about moving fast—it's about moving smart. Panic leads to trampling, separation, and mistakes. The protective role includes regulating fear, both your own and others'. In high-stress scenarios, you become the emotional anchor. Your tone of voice, body language, and commands either contribute to chaos or suppress it. That's why communication protocols are as essential as physical tactics. You must be able to give clear, simple instructions that can be followed under duress without confusion.

Commands like "Stay behind me," "Hold my belt," "Don't stop walking," or "Go left now" may seem overly simplistic in normal circumstances. But in an adrenaline-charged moment when your companions are frozen, crying, or disoriented, simplicity becomes survival. Your commands must be brief, repeatable, and delivered with unmistakable certainty. Doubt invites hesitation, and hesitation in a crisis can be fatal.

This extends beyond family to any untrained person you might be forced to protect—coworkers, students, bystanders. Your ability to project confidence, assume leadership, and maintain a structured plan under fire becomes the guiding light for others in the dark. Often, civilians are looking for someone—anyone—who seems to know what they're doing. If that's you, their survival may depend on your decisiveness.

But what happens when movement is blocked? When retreat is not an option? That's when your protective posture must evolve into a shield. In close-quarters, this might mean using your own body to block blows or prevent weapons from reaching the people behind you. It may also involve aggressive dissuasion—creating space through offensive action to regain maneuverability. Whatever the method, the outcome is singular: buy enough time for those you're protecting to escape or find cover.

Protecting others also means knowing when to separate. In some situations, you may need to instruct someone to run without you—if, for instance, you are engaged in physical defense or pinned. That decision is emotionally excruciating, but strategically sound when survival probabilities are calculated. It's why part of your preparation should include pre-planned phrases or contingency codes—short signals or gestures that indicate fallback routes, regroup locations, or distress.

Preparation for protecting others is not passive. It must be practiced, visualized, and talked through. If you live with people you intend to protect—especially spouses or children—these conversations should not be avoided. You don't need to create paranoia, but you do need to create a framework. Where do you go if you're separated? Who leads? Who calls for help? What's the phrase that signals "Get out now"? Having these in place transforms panic into procedure.

Protecting others is not about heroism—it's about controlled action in the face of chaos. It's about being the one who stays calm when everyone else can't. And when done right, it is one of the most powerful expressions of human courage and love.

7.3 Team Communication Under Fire

In any crisis involving violence or immediate danger, communication becomes both more critical and more fragile. The body floods with adrenaline, auditory exclusion may narrow your hearing, fine motor control slips, and language can degrade into fragmented phrases or silence. That's why in high-threat scenarios—whether military, law enforcement, or civilian self-defense—effective communication is not left to improvisation. It is trained, stripped of ambiguity, and hardened against stress.

The first component of tactical communication is the use of non-verbal signaling. In the field, military units frequently rely on hand signals to convey intentions without making noise. This practice, adapted to civilian contexts, becomes invaluable in environments where shouting may either be impossible, unsafe, or ineffective. A clenched fist raised in the air, a two-finger point, a flat palm slicing left—these gestures have universal applications when agreed upon beforehand.

But in spontaneous scenarios—where no common code exists—communication must adapt. Eye contact, assertive body language, and even intuitive gestures can convey urgency or instruction. For example, holding up an open palm toward someone can signal "stop," even without prior agreement. Pointing and then moving with confidence can serve as both instruction and leadership, prompting others to follow without verbal reinforcement.

Still, when words are necessary, they must be chosen carefully. The effects of stress on the brain can reduce verbal capacity by over 60%. That means long explanations, complex commands, or conditional language are less likely to be understood. Replace them with sharp, one- or two-word commands: "Run now," "Left side," "Stay low," "Quiet," "Cover me." Each phrase should function like a trigger—prompting immediate, unambiguous action.

Team communication under fire also involves feedback loops. You don't just issue a command and hope it was heard—you look for acknowledgment. This could be a nod, a movement in the intended direction, or a repeated word. Without confirmation, you cannot assume compliance. And under fire, that assumption can cost you your safety.

When teams operate under stress, they also benefit from pre-established roles. In close-protection units, roles like "lead," "cover," "evacuate," and "medic" are clearly defined. Even in civilian scenarios, the same concept can apply. If you're with a group—friends, colleagues, family—you can assign functional roles. One person monitors children. One carries gear. One makes emergency calls. Establishing these roles before an emergency occurs allows for quicker, more coordinated responses when violence breaks out.

An often overlooked part of communication during violence is what happens afterward. Post-incident coordination is just as vital as what occurs during the event. In the minutes following a violent encounter, adrenaline remains high, cognition may be impaired, and the legal ramifications of your actions begin. This is when calm, precise communication with law enforcement and medical responders becomes essential.

You must be able to articulate what happened—what you saw, what you did, why you did it. And you must do so in a manner that is truthful, concise, and defensible. Avoid speculation, emotional elaboration, or justification. Say what you observed, what you feared, and what you had to do to survive or protect others. This communication is not only critical for establishing legal clarity but also for initiating the process of mental decompression and emotional processing.

In team settings, post-incident communication must also involve debriefing. Whether you are a family that just escaped a mugging or a group of employees who stopped an active threat, sitting down afterward to talk through what happened, what worked, and what could be improved is essential. It reinforces learning, repairs trust, and prepares you better for the unthinkable should it ever happen again.

Finally, team communication under fire requires emotional intelligence. Yelling doesn't always mean dominance. Silence doesn't always mean calm. People react differently to stress, and your ability to read their states—encourage, redirect, or stabilize—can be the difference between cohesion and collapse. It's not just about barking orders. It's about listening when needed, reassuring when possible, and stepping up when others shut down.

Clear communication is not an afterthought in survival—it is a skill as sharp as any weapon and as vital as any tactic. Without it, even the best-trained teams falter. With it, even untrained groups can survive.

Chapter 8: Escape and Evasion

"The best fight is the one you never have."

– Miyamoto Musashi

8.1 Tactical Withdrawal Principles

In the world of violence and survival, there's an often-underestimated truth: real strength lies in knowing when not to fight. There is a quiet, strategic brilliance in escape that no amount of bravado or misplaced ego can replicate. While much of self-defense training focuses on the mechanics of striking, grappling, or disarming, the art of withdrawal is perhaps the most advanced and least glorified of all. Tactical withdrawal is not cowardice—it is calculated preservation. It is the decision, in a moment of high stress, to prioritize survival over engagement, life over pride, and victory through evasion rather than domination.

Disengaging from a violent encounter is far more nuanced than simply running away. The process begins with the ability to recognize when a fight is no longer winnable—or never should be fought in the first place. A true warrior does not act on impulse but on informed instinct, reading the environment, gauging the odds, and evaluating whether continued engagement serves any purpose beyond harm. That first step—making the decision to withdraw—requires courage, clarity, and discipline.

Once that decision is made, the process of breaking contact must be methodical. In military doctrine, "break contact" is a tactical maneuver involving precise steps to exit a hostile engagement while minimizing casualties and maintaining defensive capability. These principles adapt well to civilian scenarios. Whether you're caught in a bar altercation, an ambush in a parking lot, or an escalating domestic situation, the objective is to create space, avoid pursuit, and exit without drawing further attention or retaliation.

The most critical moment in breaking contact is the transition—the second you shift from engagement to withdrawal. This is where many are caught off guard. Turning your back too early, dropping your guard, or hesitating mid-move can be catastrophic. Therefore, the first movement should be aggressive, designed to stun, distract, or momentarily disrupt the attacker's plan. This might be a sudden shove into an obstacle, a strike aimed to the eyes, or a loud command that triggers confusion. The purpose isn't to win—it's to break their focus and create a window.

Within that window, movement begins. And movement is never aimless. A tactically sound withdrawal involves knowing not just how to move but where to go. This is why situational awareness, covered in earlier chapters, is so essential. A mentally mapped environment offers you pre-identified exit points, concealment zones, and choke points to avoid. You must move with confidence, even if internally shaken, because hesitancy breeds vulnerability. Every step should bring you closer to safety and farther from danger without exposing your back unnecessarily.

In highly dangerous situations, such as being pursued by an armed attacker, covering your withdrawal becomes a necessity. This doesn't mean returning fire or engaging in a prolonged standoff. It means using the environment to your advantage—knocking over furniture, slamming doors, triggering alarms, or using vehicles, shopping carts, or barricades to interrupt pursuit. Every second gained can widen the distance between you and danger. The goal is to force your pursuer to make decisions, to slow down their advance, and to take away their ability to move freely and fast.

Covering withdrawal can also involve other people—if you're with someone who's capable, their role might shift from combat support to helping create space. Throwing objects, controlling crowds, triggering distractions—these are all valid tactics when the clock is ticking and you're under pressure to escape. The key is adaptability. No two environments offer the same tools, but every environment has something—a ledge, a door, a slope, a light switch—that can be used to your benefit.

An often-underused element of tactical withdrawal is misdirection. Humans, especially under stress, are vulnerable to assumptions. If you can manipulate those assumptions, you gain time. This might mean heading in one direction, only to double back behind cover. It could involve leaving a trail that implies movement through one exit while you've taken another. In urban settings, this could mean exiting through an emergency door, triggering an alarm that sends the attacker one way while you move in another. The more pressure you can put on their decision-making, the more you regain control.

Misdirection can also be psychological. Shouting misleading instructions to imaginary allies, throwing a backpack in one direction, or pretending to surrender only to feint and flee—these are tools rooted in psychological warfare. They require split-second timing, but when used effectively, they shift the mental momentum away from the attacker and back to you. An attacker who is uncertain is slower. A slower attacker is easier to evade.

Once distance is created, your next concern is not just running, but running smart. Tactical withdrawal must balance speed with concealment. Running in a straight line down an open corridor may feel fast, but it's also predictable. A smarter move might be weaving between cars in a parking lot, using parked vehicles as visual obstructions. Or in a residential area, ducking behind fences, cutting through alleyways, and changing elevation. The unpredictability of your path becomes a form of passive defense.

It's also important to understand when to stop running. Exhaustion leads to collapse, hyperventilation, and reduced perception. You must listen to your body while remaining aware of whether you're being followed. If you believe you've escaped immediate threat but are unsure if you were marked, finding a location to observe discreetly is essential. This may be a store with security cameras, a public building, or an open space where you can monitor movement without being easily approached.

Sometimes, evasion doesn't end when you're out of the attacker's line of sight. Persistent threats may attempt to track or pursue long after the moment of violence. This is especially true in cases involving stalking, domestic violence, or premeditated targeting. Therefore, withdrawal must transition into longer-term evasion strategy when appropriate. Changing appearance—removing identifiable clothing, altering your posture, switching your hat or mask—can reduce the chance of reidentification in the short term.

In the aftermath of tactical withdrawal, it's common to experience disorientation, emotional fallout, or mental fog. This is the body's natural response to having operated on survival mode. Your next steps must be guided not just by the physical end of the incident, but by the need to stabilize and protect yourself from further risk. This often involves contacting authorities, documenting the encounter, and seeking support. Tactical withdrawal doesn't end when you stop running. It ends when you're safe and have taken steps to prevent re-engagement.

Practicing withdrawal is just as important as practicing strikes or holds. Running through escape drills—alone or with others—conditions your body and mind to respond under pressure. It teaches you the rhythm of disengagement, the scanning of exits, the placement of feet and shoulders when breaking away. Just as martial artists repeat kata, and soldiers run contact drills, civilians must rehearse withdrawal in various scenarios. Escaping a second-story building. Navigating a packed crowd. Evading someone on foot in a residential neighborhood. The more you practice, the more likely your body will execute under duress without conscious thought.

One final truth must be acknowledged: not every escape looks clean or elegant. Sometimes, escape is messy, desperate, and improvised. It may involve injury, collateral damage, or loss. But this does not diminish its value. The measure of success is not how composed you looked while fleeing. It's that you made it out alive, with enough clarity to begin the process of recovery and reflection.

Tactical withdrawal is the mature, seasoned counterweight to the temptation of violence. It is not an abandonment of strength, but the redirection of it. Knowing when to fight is a mark of skill. Knowing when not to is a mark of wisdom. And in that knowledge lies the true heart of survival.

8.2 Urban Evasion Techniques

The urban environment presents a paradox: it offers both an abundance of cover and an overwhelming array of risks. For the prepared individual, a city can become a vast camouflage net. For the unprepared, it becomes a labyrinth of exposure. Urban evasion requires not just speed or stealth, but adaptability—reading your environment in real time, interpreting patterns, navigating chaos, and staying one step ahead of whoever or whatever pursues you.

Route selection is the foundation of all successful urban evasion. It's not simply about choosing the shortest path between two points. In fact, in most cases, the most direct route is the most dangerous. A straight line often equates to predictability, and in any pursuit scenario, predictability is a liability. The ideal route balances speed, concealment, and optionality. Concealment includes architectural cover—walls, alleys, parking structures—but also lighting conditions, foot traffic, and noise levels that mask your movement. Optionality refers to having constant alternatives: detours, alternate exits, split paths that allow you to pivot without warning. Dead ends are fatal. Any chosen route must be assessed in terms of what happens if the way forward is blocked or if the pursuer changes tactics.

Another key to choosing escape routes is your familiarity with the area. Knowing your terrain grants a serious advantage. If you're operating in your own city, memorize at least three escape corridors from your most frequented locations—your workplace, home, gym, grocery store. These corridors should avoid major intersections, blind corners, and choke points like long fences or overpasses. But if you're in unfamiliar territory, adaptability must replace familiarity. In such cases, lean on architecture: follow the natural flow of alleyways, service paths, or emergency exits. Avoid brightly lit main avenues and instead move through transitional zones—areas not designed for public lingering, such as loading docks, stairwells, and parking ramps.

In any evasion, crowds become both a shield and a risk. Used properly, crowds offer moving cover, a visual smokescreen. Blending in is more than just physical movement—it's about demeanor. The panicked runner draws attention. The calm walker, even if soaked in sweat, attracts less notice. Change your body language to match those around you. Adjust your pace. Mimic distractions—look at your phone, glance into shop windows, pause briefly to tie a shoe. But this only works if you understand the crowd itself. A tight group moving toward an event may not provide mobility. A protest, flash mob, or emergency crowd can become volatile. You must learn to read the energy of the crowd. Is it moving with rhythm or panic? Is it dense enough to hide you but loose enough to let you move? And most critically, can you navigate through it without drawing attention?

Never forget the ethical responsibility involved. Civilians are not your cover if it places them at risk. Using a crowd should never become a shield to endanger others. Evade within the space between people, not through them. Avoid stampedes or causing one. Loud behavior or sudden movement can lead to panic. Remember, the best evasion goes unnoticed not just by the pursuer, but by everyone else as well.

Transportation options in urban environments are a double-edged sword. Public transit can accelerate escape but can also become traps. Buses and subways lock you into predictable routes. Trains follow rigid timelines. Ride shares require digital interaction, and license plate identification can be traced. That said, when used with foresight, these methods can work. Hopping onto a bus unnoticed and exiting two stops later can displace you geographically without exertion. But the moment a pursuer sees you enter a vehicle, your options narrow.

Personal vehicles are faster but come with their own liabilities. If you're parked in an open lot and a pursuer is in proximity, reaching your vehicle may expose you. Additionally, if they identify your license plate, they can easily track your home address or movements. If you do use a vehicle, never flee in the direction of routine. Don't drive home, to work, or to familiar zones. Instead, take irregular paths. Use parallel streets, cut through business parks, or loop until you're certain you're not followed.

A hybrid strategy is often most effective. Escape on foot until you've broken visual contact, then shift into a vehicle or transit option. By the time you've reached the second mode of transport, you should have changed at least one visible aspect—hat, jacket, gait, posture. The combination of distance and altered profile makes re-identification exponentially harder. Constant adaptation is your greatest asset. Urban evasion is not about being invisible—it's about being unmemorable, untraceable, and unpredictable in an environment built for surveillance.

8.3 Counter-Surveillance Methods

In the realm of personal safety, the best form of defense is often recognizing when danger is assembling long before it manifests. Surveillance is the prelude to action. In the context of urban threats, surveillance is not limited to government actors or corporate entities. Criminals, stalkers, and hostile individuals often engage in rudimentary but effective surveillance—watching routines, cataloging habits, testing responses. Recognizing and disrupting this early phase is the first line of proactive defense.

Surveillance detection begins with an internal shift: viewing your own life patterns from the perspective of an observer. Begin by mentally detaching and watching yourself as if you were a target. Where do you go daily? What time do you leave? Where do you park? Do you vary your lunch spot, gym schedule, walking route? Most people fall into patterns not because they're lazy, but because it simplifies life. Yet, to an adversary, that predictability is gold. Surveillance thrives on repetition. A person who leaves the house at 8:10 every morning and parks in the same garage enters a state of predictability. That window of exposure widens with every routine left unchanged.

Detection of surveillance is not about paranoia—it's about pattern recognition. A single unfamiliar face is meaningless. A face that shows up in three different places across two days at the same distance is something else. Human surveillance relies on time-distance management. A follower may lag two cars behind.

R.A.T. Fight

A pedestrian may linger just across the street. Sometimes surveillance is stationary: a person sitting on a bench day after day with no obvious reason. Your awareness should begin with baseline analysis. Know what's normal for your environment—your neighborhood, your commute, your routines. When something deviates from that baseline, mark it mentally. Repetition is the red flag. The same person at the coffee shop and then again by your parking lot exit. A vehicle that paces your walking route but doesn't seem to belong in the neighborhood. These aren't always threats, but they demand attention.

When suspicion arises, never confront prematurely. Confirmation is key. Change direction. Double back. Use reflections in windows. Step into a store and pretend to browse. Exit out a secondary door. Observe whether the suspicious individual adjusts their path in response. Those who are trained in surveillance may use cover-for-action strategies, pretending to talk on phones, checking fake maps, or pretending to be tourists. But even skilled trackers slip when forced to adapt in real time.

Once surveillance is confirmed, the next step is disruption. The primary strategy is pattern disruption. Change your schedule. Leave earlier or later. Use different exits. Alter your clothing. Walk on the opposite side of the street. Switch grocery stores. The more unpredictable you become, the harder it is for surveillance to maintain contact or relevance. This unpredictability has a secondary effect—it increases your awareness. You start seeing your city not as background, but as terrain. You read people more closely, monitor vehicles more attentively, and spot inconsistencies where once there was routine.

Disruption is not enough on its own. You need places of temporary refuge. These are not bunkers or safe rooms. They're simply spaces where you can reset, watch, and decide your next move. A safe house concept in the modern context is more about accessibility and familiarity. It could be a trusted friend's apartment, a hotel with discrete entry points, a quiet café with line-of-sight to the street. Ideally, a safe house offers multiple exits, Wi-Fi access, basic first aid, and, most importantly, quiet. It is a place where the noise of pursuit cannot reach you. Some individuals build a network of such places mentally as they move through their city—library backrooms, business lobbies, gyms with back doors.

Technology can work for or against you here. Phones with location sharing, app tracking, or cloud-connected habits can betray your position. Disable unnecessary location services. Use cash when changing locations. Avoid checking into places online. Surveillance today is hybrid—it uses both physical tracking and digital breadcrumbs. Therefore, counter-surveillance must also be dual-layered. Erase predictable habits both physically and digitally. If necessary, use burner devices or a digital hygiene strategy that limits exposure. Assume that anything habitual can be weaponized.

In the most extreme cases, particularly where threats are persistent or coordinated, professional help becomes necessary. Surveillance detection routes, practiced by executive protection agents, involve planned paths designed to expose tails. These might include looping drives, quick stops at irregular locations, and visual scans from high ground. Civilians can adapt these techniques to less conspicuous formats. Drive around a block twice. Enter a building through the front and leave through the side. Use elevators to access a different floor, then exit via stairs. Each action creates a layer of verification and, if needed, a layer of disruption.

At its core, counter-surveillance is a mindset. It's the belief that your safety is your responsibility, that observation can save you before violence has a chance to act. It's not about living in fear—it's about living with awareness. In a world where cameras are everywhere and observation is part of life, you must become fluent in the language of seeing and being seen. Master that, and your profile disappears into the noise. Fail to learn it, and your patterns write your obituary long before any physical confrontation occurs.

Chapter 9: Legal and Ethical Considerations

"The law is not a light for you or any man to see by; the law is not an instrument of any kind. The law is a causeway upon which, so long as he keeps to it, a citizen may walk safely."
— Robert Bolt

9.1 Self-Defense Law Fundamentals

Violence in self-defense is a subject that lives at the crossroads of moral philosophy, legal interpretation, and human survival. In training to protect oneself or others, it is easy to become enamored with technique, scenarios, and tactics, forgetting that the moment violence is employed—justified or not—it becomes subject to the scrutiny of the law. Understanding self-defense laws is not simply about avoiding criminal charges; it is about ensuring that your survival does not come at the cost of your future liberty. The consequences of getting it wrong can be catastrophic, even if you were morally or tactically in the right. Therefore, legal literacy is not optional—it is integral.

At the heart of all self-defense statutes lies the doctrine of *reasonable force*. This concept is both straightforward and maddeningly subjective. It asks a deceptively simple question: Would a reasonable person, standing in your shoes, believe that force—possibly even lethal force—was necessary to prevent death, serious injury, or a violent felony? This standard is interpreted through a variety of legal precedents that vary slightly by jurisdiction, but the core remains relatively stable across most Western legal systems.

What complicates this standard is context. For example, a person being punched in a parking lot may not have legal justification to use a weapon, even if they feel threatened. On the other hand, a person being cornered in their own home by a knife-wielding intruder would likely be seen as justified in using deadly force. The context is key: the location, the behavior of the aggressor, any attempts to de-escalate, and the immediacy of the perceived threat all contribute to what the court determines to be "reasonable."

Understanding how courts interpret the necessity and proportionality of force is essential. Force must be proportionate to the threat. If someone grabs your shirt and shoves you, drawing a firearm and firing might be viewed not as self-defense, but as criminal aggression. This is where people often misunderstand the implications of carrying weapons for defense: the presence of a weapon does not broaden your legal rights. If anything, it narrows your margin for error.

Many jurisdictions impose a *duty to retreat* before using force, especially lethal force. The principle behind this requirement is rooted in the idea that life is sacred and should not be taken if any alternative exists. In practice, this means that if you can safely escape a violent situation without using force—especially deadly force—you are legally obligated to do so. Failing to retreat when it is safe to do so may convert an otherwise defensible act of violence into a prosecutable offense. The question then becomes: was it possible, practical, and safe to retreat?

Importantly, not every region enforces this principle uniformly. Some areas have adopted variations of "Stand Your Ground" laws, which remove the duty to retreat in public places where one is lawfully present. These laws can be both empowering and dangerous. While they allow individuals to defend themselves without fleeing, they also place them under intense legal scrutiny if their decision to stand and fight leads to serious harm or death.

Prosecutors often dissect every second of an encounter, asking whether the defender could have stepped back, turned away, or chosen another route. Video evidence, eyewitness testimony, and forensic details become critical in such cases.

Another major legal principle is the *Castle Doctrine*, which fundamentally alters the landscape of self-defense law by asserting that a person's home is their sanctuary. Under this doctrine, individuals are generally not required to retreat when faced with an intruder in their residence. The legal presumption is that a person breaking into your home is doing so with malicious intent, and as such, your use of force—potentially even deadly force—is more likely to be justified without question.

Some jurisdictions expand this doctrine beyond the home to include vehicles or places of business. The rationale is the same: within your private domain, your right to security outweighs the intruder's right to life once they have violated that space. However, even in these cases, nuances matter. If, for example, you invite someone into your home and a dispute escalates, the Castle Doctrine may no longer apply. Courts will consider whether the perceived threat justified the level of force used and whether the intruder had the legal status of a guest.

It's crucial to note that legal protections also depend on how quickly and transparently you report the incident. A legitimate self-defense case can be undermined if the defender flees the scene, hides evidence, or refuses to cooperate with law enforcement. These actions can be interpreted as consciousness of guilt, even if the original act was legally justified. Immediate, clear communication with law enforcement, ideally accompanied by legal representation, is the safest course of action.

The aftermath of a violent self-defense encounter is not just a legal issue—it is also psychological. Many people assume that surviving the encounter is the end of the battle. In truth, it may be the beginning of a legal saga that lasts months or even years. Prosecutors may file charges despite clear evidence of justification, often due to public pressure, political considerations, or simply differing interpretations of the event. In these cases, your understanding of self-defense law, and how well you followed its principles, can mean the difference between freedom and incarceration.

The use of weapons adds another layer of complexity. In many jurisdictions, the legality of your defensive actions is contingent not only on your behavior during the incident but also on the legal status of the weapon itself. If you used a firearm, was it legally owned and carried? Was it concealed or openly carried according to state laws? If you used a knife or blunt object, was it considered a weapon under the local definition, and were you authorized to possess it? Ignorance of weapon laws can undo an otherwise justified act of self-defense.

Moreover, the law also distinguishes between different classes of threats. A credible threat of rape, kidnapping, or serious bodily harm can justify the use of force. But verbal threats alone, without accompanying physical action or ability to carry them out, usually fall short of the standard required to use force in return. Therefore, while the law does not expect perfection in decision-making during moments of intense fear or danger, it does require that actions be grounded in credible, observable threats.

In civil law, even a criminal acquittal doesn't guarantee peace. Victims of force may sue the defender for damages, alleging excessive violence, emotional trauma, or wrongful injury. Civil suits operate under different standards of proof and can be devastating even to those who acted entirely within the law. This dual risk—criminal and civil—underscores the importance of not only knowing the law but following it rigorously under pressure.

In some situations, the presence of surveillance cameras, witness statements, or even body-worn cameras (as used by many self-defense instructors or private security personnel) can offer clarity and protection. However, these tools cut both ways. If your behavior on camera contradicts your testimony or legal justification, it will be used against you.

Lastly, training is not just about physical readiness—it should include a deep understanding of your jurisdiction's specific self-defense laws. These can be taught by experienced defense attorneys, law enforcement liaisons, or reputable self-defense programs. Ignorance is not a defense, and neither is good intent. The courtroom does not judge the morality of your actions in isolation—it weighs them against the legal statutes of your state or country, filtered through the lens of precedent, interpretation, and the credibility of your account.

In sum, understanding the fundamentals of self-defense law is not an accessory to your training—it is the compass by which every decision should be guided. Your ability to make split-second choices under stress must be matched by your ability to justify them clearly and confidently in a legal setting. Being skilled is not enough. You must also be lawful. The truly prepared defender is not just one who can win the fight, but one who can walk away—both from the scene and from the courtroom—with freedom intact.

9.2 Documentation and Evidence

The moments following a violent encounter are often saturated with adrenaline, confusion, and emotional disarray. Yet it is precisely during these moments—or shortly thereafter—that the most crucial decisions must be made to protect not just one's physical safety, but their legal standing. Documenting a violent incident is not an abstract concern for bureaucratic clarity; it is the foundation upon which your legal defense will either stand solid or crumble under scrutiny. In the court of law, what happened matters far less than what can be *proven* to have happened.

After any use of force in a self-defense situation, your immediate priority is to ensure personal safety. Once that is established and the threat is neutralized or withdrawn, the next imperative is to contact law enforcement. Even if no charges are eventually filed, failing to report the event promptly can raise red flags. Prosecutors, juries, and judges often equate silence or delay with guilt. A person who truly acted in self-defense should be willing—if not eager—to explain the circumstances, provided they do so within the protection of sound legal counsel.

When speaking to law enforcement, it is critical to understand the fine line between cooperation and self-incrimination. The Fifth Amendment exists for a reason. Ideally, your first contact with police should be a calm, minimal statement that identifies you as the victim, establishes that you were attacked, and confirms that you defended yourself in fear for your life. Beyond that, you should explicitly request an attorney before offering further details. Anything you say can and will be used, and when delivered under duress or emotional turmoil, even truthful statements can be twisted.

Once the scene is secured and law enforcement is present, documentation must begin immediately—especially if the police are not already doing it to the level of detail your situation requires. If it is safe to do so, you should take photos or videos of the scene, your injuries, your clothing, any weapons used, and any damage to the surroundings that supports your version of events. These images may later prove invaluable, especially if there are conflicting witness statements or attempts by the attacker (or their associates) to fabricate a different narrative.

Eyewitnesses can be the linchpin in a self-defense case. Human memory is fallible, and it degrades rapidly under stress. Identifying witnesses at the scene, asking for their names and contact information, and ideally recording their initial impressions—either through notes or discreet video (if permissible)—can preserve clarity before memories shift. The more you can tie their accounts to real-time documentation, the harder it is for alternate versions of the story to take root.

It is important to understand that not all witnesses are equal. Eyewitnesses who were neutral bystanders carry more weight than friends or family members who may be perceived as biased. Likewise, individuals with no connection to either party, especially those who are articulate and willing to speak clearly in court, are particularly valuable. If the scene attracted a crowd, try to identify anyone who was recording. Video footage—especially from third-party phones, surveillance cameras, or nearby dashcams—can serve as an objective record that transcends interpretation.

Physical evidence must be treated as both fragile and sacred. Blood trails, shell casings, broken objects, drag marks—these details may speak volumes to trained forensic investigators, but they can also be quickly altered, destroyed, or cleaned up if you're not careful. Avoid disturbing the scene unnecessarily, but do make mental or photographic notes of anything that might later be contested. For instance, if your attacker dropped a weapon or made a verbal threat, those elements must be recorded as soon as possible, even if the object is removed or the words denied later.

Your own injuries must be medically evaluated and documented without delay. This serves two purposes. First, it ensures your health and rules out any internal trauma you may not initially detect. Second, it provides a professional, third-party record that corroborates the level of force you claim was used against you.

Emergency room staff or urgent care clinics are accustomed to handling such cases and often include useful language in their reports that can later support your legal narrative.

In the days following the incident, begin organizing your documentation into a coherent timeline. Write a personal account while the memory is fresh, noting specific times, actions, threats, and responses. Keep it factual and avoid emotional embellishment. Include everything that might later be questioned, even if it seems insignificant. If you can, recreate the layout of the scene from memory—drawings, maps, or digital diagrams can aid your attorney and may be used in court.

Legal proceedings move slowly, and memories fade. Proper documentation is your safeguard against time, interpretation, and manipulation. In the end, justice often favors the prepared, not merely the righteous.

9.3 Moral and Psychological Aftermath

While physical self-defense is immediate, visceral, and often explosive, its psychological consequences unfold more gradually—like tremors that follow a quake. It is easy to believe that once the attacker is neutralized and the threat gone, the ordeal is over. But for many defenders, especially those unaccustomed to violence, the emotional and ethical reverberations can persist for months or even years.

The moral dimension of defensive violence is complex. On the surface, it seems straightforward: you did what you had to do to survive. But deeper reflection often stirs unease. Was it necessary to hit that hard, to keep going after the threat began to retreat, or to use a weapon when fists might have sufficed? These are questions that will return unbidden at quiet moments, and the answers may not always be comforting. This is why a clear framework for ethical decision-making must be established before an incident ever occurs.

Your values, your sense of justice, and your commitment to preserving life must all be integrated into your training and mindset. Violence in self-defense is not about punishing evil—it is about preserving your life and the lives of those you are obligated to protect. The moment you allow anger, revenge, or ego to dictate your response, you step outside the boundaries of ethical self-defense and risk not just legal consequences, but profound psychological damage.

The aftermath of a violent encounter often includes a deep questioning of identity. People who saw themselves as peaceful, law-abiding citizens may struggle with the fact that they were capable of inflicting harm—even lethal harm. They may wrestle with guilt, anxiety, depression, or even symptoms of post-traumatic stress disorder. Nightmares, flashbacks, irritability, and emotional numbness are not uncommon. These responses are not signs of weakness; they are evidence that you are still human.

It is essential to seek support during this period. Professional counseling from therapists familiar with trauma, especially those who understand self-defense or combat-related issues, can provide a safe environment to process what happened. Talking with others who have been through similar experiences can also offer perspective and reduce feelings of isolation. Suppressing these emotions in the name of toughness or stoicism is not only harmful—it can exacerbate the long-term impact and delay healing.

Social relationships can also become strained in the aftermath of justified violence. Friends or coworkers who don't understand the context may view you differently. Some may avoid you, others may over-glorify what you did, turning it into a kind of legend you don't want to live in. You may become the subject of gossip or suspicion, especially in smaller communities or tightly knit circles. People love stories, and your experience—particularly if it involved visible violence or media attention—may be reshaped by others for their own purposes.

Family members may also react in unexpected ways. Some will express pride, others concern. Children may be frightened, confused, or curious in ways that are difficult to manage. If your defensive actions took place in their presence, they may carry their own emotional scars. Addressing their fears and emotions openly, without shame or avoidance, is critical for their development and for the family's recovery as a whole.

Public perception can be especially volatile if the incident receives media coverage or online scrutiny. In the digital age, any act of violence—no matter how justified—can become a polarizing topic. Strangers who know nothing of your character or the context may take sides based on ideology, race, or simple misinterpretation. It can be deeply unsettling to find your name associated with controversy, especially when your intent was never to harm, only to survive.

To navigate this, clarity of conscience is essential. You must return to the truth of your actions and the values that guided them. Were you defending life, or indulging in violence? Were your decisions born of fear or fury? The more you understand your own motives, the more resilient you will be to criticism, misunderstanding, or public judgment.

Ultimately, the moral and psychological recovery from a violent encounter is a process, not a destination. It may involve grief—not just for the harm done, but for the innocence lost. It may include shame, pride, doubt, and clarity, all braided into the same emotional rope. You may question your identity, your choices, and your future. This is not unusual. It is the cost of being fully human in moments when humanity is tested.

The path forward requires grace, patience, and honesty. It requires the courage to confront not just an external threat, but the internal fallout of survival. Self-defense does not end when the attacker is gone. It continues in the courtroom, in the mind, and in the mirror. The ultimate goal is not just to be alive, but to live well—with integrity, understanding, and peace.

Chapter 10: Training and Skill Development

"Train like you fight, fight like you train." — U.S. Military Doctrine

10.1 Physical Conditioning Programs

True preparation for violent encounters does not begin with techniques—it begins with the body. No matter how refined your skillset, how sharp your awareness, or how disciplined your mindset, you remain a biological being subject to the same physiological laws as anyone else. Strength, speed, stamina, mobility, and resilience are the physical currencies that underlie every defensive action. Without them, strategy collapses into wishful thinking. Without them, training is theory, not practice. The body is your first and last weapon.

Combat-specific conditioning does not look like the routines you find in commercial gyms or wellness retreats. It is not built for aesthetics or longevity alone. It is engineered for explosive performance under stress, for sustained endurance through chaos, and for recovery in the aftermath of violence. It is not a question of merely being "in shape"; it is a question of being operationally ready for the worst-case scenario—a scenario in which your life or someone else's may depend on your ability to act without hesitation and move with controlled aggression.

The demands of a real-world violent encounter are dynamic and unpredictable. You may be forced to sprint across uneven terrain, carry a wounded loved one, grapple on concrete, or fight off multiple attackers in tight quarters. You may have to recover quickly from a fall, regain balance after a blow, or maintain a defensive posture under fatigue. The body must be trained to operate not under perfect conditions but under the most compromised ones—under stress, pain, confusion, and exhaustion. This is the core of combat-specific fitness: functional ability in adverse conditions.

A proper conditioning regimen begins with the development of foundational strength. This is not the bloated muscle of bodybuilding, but the kind of raw, practical strength that allows you to lift, pull, strike, and resist with control. Deadlifts, sandbag carries, weighted drags, and pull-up variations create a neuromuscular foundation that prepares you to move with purpose and power. You're not training to look strong. You're training to *be* strong where it counts—in your core, your grip, your back, and your legs.

Just as critical is explosive power. In a violent confrontation, milliseconds matter. The ability to generate sudden force—a knee to the groin, a push that creates space, a sprint to an exit—requires plyometric capacity. Jump squats, medicine ball throws, and kettlebell swings simulate this kind of output. These movements recruit fast-twitch muscle fibers, which are the difference between reacting in time and reacting too late. In street violence, there is rarely a second chance.

Yet raw strength and power without mobility is a liability. Flexibility and joint range of motion determine whether you can move fluidly, avoid injury, and execute techniques effectively. Functional flexibility does not mean sitting in a split or holding a yoga pose for minutes on end—it means being able to drop into a low stance, pivot quickly, raise your arms overhead without strain, and rotate your hips under pressure. A blend of dynamic stretching, full-range movement drills, and joint mobility routines must become a daily habit. Think of it as lubricating the machine before turning it on.

Cardiovascular conditioning must not be confused with endurance jogging or casual aerobics. In combat, the heart rate does not rise steadily—it spikes and crashes unpredictably. Intervals, sprints, circuits, and simulated combat rounds are better tools for this kind of adaptation. You must be able to perform at near-maximal heart rate and recover quickly, again and again. A healthy heart and vascular system not only support your survival in the moment—they also determine how well you recover afterward.

Balance and proprioception—the body's sense of its position in space—are often overlooked in self-defense circles, yet they form the invisible glue that binds all movement. A punch thrown from an unstable platform loses power. A retreat that stumbles over uneven ground becomes a liability. Training barefoot, using unstable surfaces, integrating single-leg drills, and practicing dynamic changes in direction build an internal gyroscope that helps you stay upright and mobile when the ground itself is against you.

Then there is the matter of injury prevention. Training for violence without regard for bodily wear is the fastest path to failure. It is not enough to push hard. You must also train smart. Weak points—ankles, knees, shoulders, lower back—must be strengthened with deliberate attention. This means tendon and ligament training, eccentric loading to build durability, and prehabilitation exercises that ensure long-term performance. The goal is not to avoid all stress. The goal is to expose the body to controlled stress so that it learns to absorb, redirect, and recover from it.

Part of this involves understanding the difference between good pain and bad pain. Discomfort is a natural part of growth. Injury is not. A well-rounded physical program includes intelligent deloading phases, rest cycles, and alternative modalities like cold immersion, breathwork, massage therapy, or even stillness. The nervous system, like a soldier, cannot remain on high alert forever. It must reset.

As the body ages, training must evolve—not weaken, but become more precise. A younger athlete may rely on sheer recovery capacity. An older one must rely on economy, posture, timing, and refined mechanics. Defensive capability should not decay with age; it should mature. A man in his sixties should still be able to strike hard, move efficiently, and think clearly under pressure. This is not fantasy—it is the reward of sustained, intelligent conditioning.

Mental resilience is born, in part, from physical resilience. When your body knows that it has been tested, pushed, and proven, your mind trusts it. You do not freeze in fear wondering if you can perform—you move, because your muscles remember. Physical training is not just preparation for violence. It is the antidote to self-doubt.

To be clear, training does not require a warehouse gym or expensive equipment. Much can be accomplished with bodyweight, resistance bands, a few weights, and creativity. What matters is consistency, intensity, and intent. A five-day-a-week gym-goer who trains like a civilian will remain a civilian in spirit. A three-day-a-week practitioner who trains like their life depends on it will be infinitely more prepared when it does.

The defensive athlete must also understand that perfection is not the goal. There is no ideal body type, no single benchmark that defines readiness. Each body has its own assets and limitations. A smaller person may be faster. A larger person may strike harder. The key is not to match someone else's profile but to master your own. You must know what you can do, what you can't, and how to close the gap through effort, adaptation, and will.

Finally, every training session is a vote. A vote for strength over fragility. For capability over dependence. For survival over victimhood. It is easy to train when it's convenient. It is meaningful to train when it isn't. Violence doesn't arrive on a schedule. Neither should your readiness. And while most people will never be forced to use their body to defend themselves or their family, those who train live with the quiet confidence that if that day ever comes, they will not meet it as prey—but as someone ready to fight, endure, and win.

10.2 Skill Acquisition and Retention

Mastery in self-defense is not born from theory, nor from occasional bursts of enthusiasm. It is built through the painstaking accumulation of ingrained responses—reactions that bypass hesitation and emerge fluidly under pressure. To reach that point, the defender must engage with how humans actually learn physical skills: not just to perform them when calm, but to access them when the stakes are real, the heart is pounding, and milliseconds count.

The cornerstone of this process is motor learning. This term is often misunderstood in the context of self-defense, where people sometimes confuse knowing a technique with owning it. Knowledge is conceptual. Ownership is neurological. A move you've read about, watched, or practiced once or twice is still a stranger in your nervous system. A move you've drilled repeatedly in realistic context becomes a reflex—embedded in muscle memory and retrieved without conscious effort. The goal of any serious practitioner should be to develop a library of such automatic responses, each one tailored to the real-world violence scenarios most relevant to their environment and physicality.

Muscle memory isn't confined to muscles, of course. It is a function of the brain—specifically, the cerebellum and basal ganglia, which store and refine motor patterns through repetition and feedback. When a technique is introduced to the body, the first attempts are clumsy, often inefficient. Neural pathways are firing for the first time, and the brain is unsure which muscles to activate, which to relax, how much force is needed, or how to sequence the motion. Over time, with repeated, mindful practice, those pathways become streamlined. What once required thought becomes instinct. But it must be deliberate. Sloppy repetition engrains sloppy performance. Practicing slowly and precisely, especially in the early stages, creates a foundation of control that later accelerates into usable speed.

This is where many self-defense programs falter—they teach too many techniques without investing enough time in functional retention. It is far better to have five reflexive, high-percentage techniques that survive stress than fifty memorized moves that evaporate under adrenaline. That's why skill curation is vital. Focus on movements that fit your body type, your legal and environmental context, and your likely threat scenarios. Then drill them until they are as familiar as walking.

But the most significant variable is stress. All skill development must eventually pass through the crucible of pressure testing. There is a stark difference between performing a disarm drill in a cooperative training environment and executing that same movement when your heart rate is spiking, your hands are trembling, and your vision is tunneled from adrenaline. The physiological effects of stress are profound—fine motor skills degrade, decision-making slows, and the body reverts to its deepest habits. If those habits are not forged in stress-inoculated training, they simply won't hold.

Stress testing doesn't have to mimic the brutality of real violence, but it must simulate its psychological conditions. This can be done through surprise drills, elevated heart rate scenarios, low-light environments, or roleplaying exercises with verbal escalation and shifting dynamics. The key is to train the brain to function through confusion, fear, and uncertainty. When you can still perform under that pressure—even imperfectly—you're converting training into survivability.

Of course, no training routine is immune to life's interruptions. Illness, travel, work obligations, or injury can sideline even the most committed practitioner. This is where skill degradation management becomes crucial. Like any physical capacity, unused defensive skills will erode. But erosion can be slowed, and sometimes reversed quickly, with strategic interventions.

Visualization is a powerful tool in this context. Rehearsing techniques mentally—seeing and feeling them vividly in your mind—activates many of the same neural pathways as physical practice. While it cannot replace contact training, it maintains the motor pattern and keeps the brain fluent in sequencing. Short movement snacks—five to ten-minute daily drills, even in confined spaces—also stave off decay. Practicing movement flows, grip transitions, or footwork patterns keeps the machinery primed until full training resumes.

Some skills, particularly those involving timing and contact—like striking or grappling—require reintroduction through live feedback. In such cases, the key is not to rush back to peak performance, but to recalibrate. Accept that your edge has dulled, and approach the first sessions back as re-entry, not testing grounds. With the right approach, most trained individuals recover their defensive fluency faster than they acquired it the first time. The pattern is still there—just waiting to be reactivated.

Consistency, not perfection, determines whether a skill survives. Training doesn't need to be heroic every session. It simply needs to be regular, relevant, and reality-based. The body learns what it does often. If violence is something you may someday face, your training must respect that possibility through repetition and resilience.

10.3 Continuous Improvement Systems

Training is never finished. Skill acquisition is not a destination but a constantly shifting terrain. As your body changes, your environment shifts, your legal awareness deepens, and your understanding of violence evolves, your training must adapt in parallel. That is why continuous improvement is not just a philosophy—it's a functional necessity. Without feedback, measurement, and refinement, even the most rigorous program becomes stagnant, vulnerable, and eventually, ineffective.

The first component of sustainable improvement is tracking. What gets measured gets improved. This doesn't mean obsessing over fitness data or turning your training into spreadsheets, but it does mean developing a personal benchmark system. How quickly can you draw and deploy a tool from concealment? How effectively can you transition from verbal de-escalation to physical movement? How long can you maintain output under stress before your technique breaks down? These are measurable variables. Over time, recording your performance under varied conditions gives you a real-time map of progress—and reveals plateaus or regressions before they become liabilities.

These metrics are not about comparison with others, but comparison with your former self. They offer clarity about what is improving and what isn't. Are you faster, more accurate, more composed under pressure? Or are you simply repeating drills without adaptation? Once you identify performance gaps, you can target them precisely. This tight feedback loop transforms training from a routine into a constantly calibrated survival system.

No system of improvement is complete without the right partners. Training with others introduces complexity, unpredictability, and realism that solo practice cannot replicate. But not all training partners are equal. The best ones challenge you without ego, provide honest feedback, and force you to adapt without injury. They resist realistically, they attack creatively, and they help you find weaknesses you didn't know existed.

The wrong partners—those who go too hard, try to "win" in training, or don't respect boundaries—are worse than no partner at all. They breed bad habits, fear of injury, or distorted expectations about what real violence entails. Select partners who match your goals and respect the mission: improving survival skills, not proving superiority. In ideal setups, you train with people who vary in size, strength, and style. This diversity forces your techniques to become adaptable, not dependent on a single opponent profile.

When solo training is the only option, your environment becomes your teacher. But not all spaces are created equal. For self-defense preparation, you don't need high-tech facilities. You need a space where you can move freely, train with your tools, and simulate your likely threat environments. A garage, backyard, or even a cleared-out room can become a battlefield. Mats, mirrors, and heavy bags are helpful but not essential. What matters is that the space lets you move, fall, recover, and simulate chaos.

Environmental variation is also a critical component of ongoing improvement. Training in the same setting over and over creates comfort—but real violence rarely occurs in comfort zones. Practicing in darkness, on uneven terrain, in restrictive clothing, or while fatigued replicates the unpredictability of crisis. Even walking through your daily environments with a tactical mindset—identifying exits, evaluating threats, planning movement—sharpens awareness and decision-making. Improvement doesn't always require sweating. Sometimes it just requires seeing with new eyes.

Technology, used intelligently, can also support continuous development. Video analysis of your movement reveals habits and inefficiencies that feel invisible from within the motion. Slow-motion review, side-by-side comparisons, and feedback from experienced observers provide insight that you cannot achieve alone. Recording sparring sessions or drills lets you evaluate composure, reaction time, and follow-through with brutal honesty. What felt fast may look slow. What felt decisive may look hesitant. These revelations are not criticism—they are opportunities for evolution.

To avoid stagnation, periodic self-assessment must be paired with intentional disruption. This means introducing new scenarios, shifting roles, experimenting with different tools, or rotating training focus across striking, grappling, weapon retention, or escape. These cycles mirror real-life unpredictability. You don't get to choose which type of violence finds you. You can only choose to be broadly ready.

Ultimately, the path of continuous improvement in self-defense is not about reaching invincibility. It's about eliminating preventable failures, shortening your response time, and expanding your capacity to function when others freeze. It's about knowing that no matter how skilled you become, there is always a deeper layer—one more blind spot, one more adjustment, one more level of readiness to unlock.

You train not just to win, but to endure. Not just to act, but to adapt. Not just to survive, but to improve—forever.

Conclusion: The Path Forward

True strength is rarely loud. It doesn't walk with a swagger or flash its teeth at the first sign of trouble. The kind of strength cultivated through the principles in this book—Rapid Assault Tactics (R.A.T.)—is quiet, composed, and rooted in clarity. It does not seek confrontation, but it does not fear it. It is the kind of strength that walks down a dark alley not to look for danger, but because it has no other choice—and knows it can handle whatever waits at the other end.

This book has never been about teaching violence for violence's sake. The goal was never to create fighters with short tempers or civilians who mistake fear for readiness. If anything, the mission was precisely the opposite: to create people who are calm, composed, difficult to provoke, and even harder to defeat. It was about transforming the average person from a passive potential victim into an active guardian of their own safety—someone equipped not only with tools and techniques but with discernment.

Integrating R.A.T. principles into everyday life is not about walking around in a constant state of readiness, scanning every shadow, flinching at every movement. That's paranoia, and paranoia is not sustainable. What we're talking about is a lifestyle shift—a permanent reorientation of how you carry yourself, how you observe the world, and how you prepare for moments you hope will never come.

That begins with situational awareness, which isn't a switch you flip during emergencies but a habit you cultivate in ordinary life. You don't need to obsessively monitor every corner or live in fear of ambushes. What you need is a cultivated baseline of alertness—a relaxed but attentive state in which you remain aware of exits, note anomalies, and quietly map out your environment. Over time, this becomes second nature. You begin to "see" differently. You sense tension in people's posture. You notice when someone's path doesn't align with their apparent intent. You detect subtle patterns. This doesn't make you paranoid. It makes you present.

But awareness without readiness is hollow. That's why physical training—consistent, focused, purposeful—is essential. You must train as if you will need it tomorrow while hoping that you never will. You must be able to run, to fight, to fall, to recover, and to make decisions under stress. But beyond the mechanics of movement, you must train your will. Your resolve. Your ability to choose action over hesitation. This kind of readiness is not only physical but psychological. It means rehearsing scenarios in your mind, visualizing your responses, and inoculating yourself against fear through exposure, not avoidance.

Yet all of this—awareness, readiness, decisiveness—must live within a moral framework. That is the defining mark of the responsible practitioner. The ability to harm must be matched by the wisdom not to. Violence, even justified violence, carries consequences. Legal, emotional, spiritual. You must know the law. You must know your rights. And you must also know your own values. You must train not just for effectiveness but for restraint. Knowing when *not* to engage is just as vital as knowing how.

This is what it means to carry power without becoming consumed by it. The temptation, once skill and confidence grow, is to begin seeing the world through the lens of potential violence. Every rude gesture becomes a test. Every disagreement becomes a battlefield. That's not strength. That's weakness wearing the mask of toughness. The mature warrior knows that the greatest victory is often in the confrontation that never escalates. The argument that never became a fight. The aggressive man in the parking lot who was met with calm, unshakable presence, and then backed off.

This is where verbal de-escalation enters. The ability to control a situation with words, body language, and energy is not separate from the physical training—it is an extension of it. A person who has trained their body and mind to deal with violence rarely needs to prove anything to anyone. They don't escalate because they don't have to. And paradoxically, that is often what ends the threat. Predators look for prey, not other predators. The person who radiates composure, awareness, and readiness is rarely tested.

But let's be clear: readiness is not a guarantee. No amount of training can eliminate danger entirely. Violence is chaotic, unfair, and often blindsides even the most prepared. What training gives you is not control over the world, but control over *yourself* within the world. It gives you options. It gives you time. It gives you a chance. And in a violent encounter, even one extra second, one extra inch, one extra decision, can mean the difference between survival and tragedy.

Integrating R.A.T. into your life also means thinking beyond yourself. Once you begin to see with clear eyes—once you've stepped out of the fog that most people walk through daily—you start to take responsibility not only for your safety, but for those around you. Your family. Your friends. Even strangers, in some cases. You move differently in public spaces. You sit where you can see the door. You notice the man who's acting erratically before anyone else does. You walk with your loved ones positioned inside your protective arc. You don't just prepare to fight—you prepare to *shield*.

But this responsibility must never harden into aggression. The point of R.A.T. is not to make you more dangerous—it's to make you *less* vulnerable. And the best self-defense is still avoidance.

Escape. De-escalation. The use of violence must always be a last resort—not because you're afraid of it, but because you *respect* it. Every violent act, even when justified, sends shockwaves through your life. Legally, yes. But also psychologically. Spiritually. If you can walk away without using force, and still remain safe, that is the highest expression of mastery.

At the end of this journey, you are not just stronger, faster, or more aware. You are wiser. You know that being hard to kill is not the same as being hard to live with. You've cultivated not just defensive capabilities but a lifestyle of readiness—one that is quietly embedded in everything you do. How you walk. How you scan. How you train. How you speak. You've become someone who does not seek conflict, but does not shrink from it either. Someone who stands up not out of pride, but out of principle. Someone who doesn't just protect themselves—but embodies the presence of safety for others.

This path is not easy. It demands effort, consistency, and humility. It asks you to confront your fears, your limits, and sometimes your own instincts. It means living in a way that most people never will—prepared, aware, restrained, and lethal only when absolutely necessary. But the reward is immense. Not just survival. Not just safety. But the deep internal peace that comes from knowing: if the moment ever comes, you are ready.

This is the true goal of Rapid Assault Tactics. Not to make you paranoid. Not to make you violent. But to make you capable. Clear. Calm. And free.

Because in the end, the best fight is still the one you never have.

www.ingramcontent.com/pod-product-compliance
Lightning Source LLC
Chambersburg PA
CBHW070556170426
43201CB00012B/1862